'Today there is no denying or avoiding the challenge for the Church. There is no lack of diagnosis, analysis and commentary on what we face and what must be done. As necessary and well-meaning as such interventions are, I am most stimulated and persuaded by those whose voice speaks Christianly.

'Hannah's is such a voice; a profound, learned, informed, committed, invested and hope-filled voice. I am delighted she has written *Living His Story Together* – I can't think of any follower of Jesus who won't be inspired and motivated by it. For it sets before us a vision of the local church that engages in the ministry of Christ Jesus in the power of the Spirit. Hannah does not deal in ideals or theory, but in practice and engagement – with the living God and his life among us. It's a book to renew us and revive us – because in actual fact it is a book about God. As I read this my head lifted and my heart was strengthened as I encountered the gospel; Jesus is the hope for the Church – and if we take notice of this book, it is Jesus' ways and means which we will faithfully witness to.'
Justin Welby, Archbishop of Canterbury

'Hannah Steele is a gifted communicator, a deep thinker about mission and a passionate evangelist. It's hard to imagine a better person to write on the Church as it engages the world, and this book does not disappoint – it is full of new angles, wise perspectives and rich reflection.'
Bishop Graham Tomlin

'Two of the greatest and gravest crises that grip our society are hopelessness and isolation. Our world desperately needs community and the good news of Jesus. That is why Hannah Steele's wonderful book is so timely. *Living His Story Together* masterfully unpacks what it means to be a gospel-centred, Spirit-filled, prayer-soaked, creativity-unleashing, culturally relevant body of believers. It is deeply researched, unashamedly biblical, discerningly strategic and intensely practical. Packed with personal stories, winsome humour, serious theologians and an abundance of references to TV shows and boxsets, I am excited by the potential of this book to inspire

and shape us into a Church that readily and fruitfully responds in word and deed to the needs of today.'
Phil Knox, missiologist and author, Evangelical Alliance

'Christian mission is no longer limited to specific places – from here to there – but is now global to everywhere for everyone called to follow Jesus Christ. This insightful book explores the Church's mission in a world far from Christian influence. Using stories, examining historical connotations of mission and the need to listen to those adversely affected by them, Hannah illustrates the powerful impact of community when living out biblical concepts of mission together. She suggests practical ways to be Christ's missionary disciples in a changing cultural context. It is an inspiring resource for any church community that seeks to live out faith with a strong sense of purpose and joy as a witness to God's love in the world.'
The Revd Canon Dr Sharon Prentis, Deputy Director of the Racial Justice Unit

LIVING HIS STORY TOGETHER

Being a community of missionary disciples

Hannah Steele

First published in Great Britain in 2024

SPCK
SPCK Group
Studio 101
The Record Hall
16–16A Baldwin's Gardens
London EC1N 7RJ

www.spck.org.uk

British Library Cataloguing-in-Publication Data
A catalogue record for this book is available from the British Library.

ISBN: 978-0-281-08726-6
eBook: 978-0-281-08727-3

Typeset by Fakenham Prepress Solutions, Fakenham, Norfolk NR21 8NL
First printed in Great Britain by Clays Ltd, Bungay, Suffolk

eBook by Fakenham Prepress Solutions, Fakenham, Norfolk NR21 8NL

For the women who prayed

Copyright acknowledgements

Contents

Acknowledgements

Every book is a labour of love and not only by the one who writes it. When Archbishop Justin asked me to be the author of his Lent Book for 2021, *Living His Story*, I never imagined I could produce something that would be read by so many, and I continue to be grateful for that opportunity. This follow-on book includes much I wish I had said back then, as well as things that have since emerged and developed in my thinking.

I am grateful to St Mellitus College for space in the summer of 2023 to spend time writing and to the students (past and present) who have willingly shared their stories with me. They and their ministry fill me with hope for the Church.

Alison Barr at SPCK has been a constant source of encouragement and wisdom and it has been a joy to work with her again on this book.

Heartfelt thanks go to All Saints Peckham, the church community I have been part of for twenty-five years. The various clergy (Bob, Frog, Jonathan and Jenny) have encouraged my faith and my ministry in different ways. Being part of a vibrant and diverse community that seeks to live missionally and compassionately has been an immense privilege, and it has been home to me and my family through the ups and downs of life. I am thankful to Nesta and Guerline for reminding me of a story I knew so well but heard afresh through their voices and prayers.

Lastly, my thanks go to my husband Gavin whose labour of love this has also been. Without his endless patience and generosity, I doubt I would ever have finished the book. As I was nearing the final stages of writing, my dear friend and fellow encourager in all things missional church, Chris Lane, sent me the following quote by Frederick Buechner. He thought of me when he read it and knew I would love it, and he was right. It says everything I could hope to say about why the task of mission is so vital for the Church:

> In the last analysis, you cannot pontificate but only point. A Christian is who points at Christ and says, 'I can't prove a thing, but there's something about his eyes and his voice. There's something about the way he carries his head, his hands, the way he carries his cross – the way he carries me.'[1]

Introduction

My father was ordained in the 1960s and took up his curacy at a parish church in Folkestone. It was in a beautiful setting with wide views out to sea. The church was traditional and strongly liturgical and one of the challenges my dad faced when he was ordained priest was singing the eucharistic prayer. Not known for his perfect pitch, he had an agreement with the organist that he would play a single note as the cue for Dad to begin, 'The Lord is here'.

One winter's morning, dressed in liturgical robes, my father stood at the altar with his arms outstretched, inclined his ear and launched into a somewhat deep, 'The Lord is here'. At this point the organist turned and looked at him in shock as he had not yet played a note. My dad had, in fact, taken his cue from the foghorn of a ship coming into harbour.

A humorous story perhaps, but one that illustrates a serious point. Where does the Church take its cue from? Fast forward fifty years and the world outside its walls is changing rapidly. How are we to respond? Do we carry on with business as usual, preserving the faith, or are we required to listen and respond and even adapt to what we see and hear around us?

It is frequently said that the Church in the West is at crisis point. Decline in terms of church attendance was revealed in the 2021 Census, with statistics showing that the number of people ticking the 'Christian' box was 46.2%, the first time the figure has fallen below 50% of the population, and that more people attend the mosque each week than their local parish church.[1] The greatest area of increase is in the 'nones' – those who profess to no religion at all – which has tripled since the millennium to 37%.

The church I am part of in Peckham in south-east London was built in 1867 because existing churches could not cater for the expanding population. This, of course, was an era when 'going to church' was simply what most people did. Now, as many of those vast and glorious Victorian buildings stand empty or are turned into desirable flats for city workers, office spaces or performance venues, it can be hard for the Church to know how to navigate such a complex change.

In August 2023, *The Times* newspaper revealed the results of a survey of just over a thousand Anglican clergy in active ministry.[2] When asked whether they thought their church would still be holding a regular Sunday service in ten years' time, 64.8% considered that either likely or very likely, whereas 20.5% thought it to be unlikely, with some commenting that their regular Sunday services had already ceased. Of clergy interviewed, 76.8% predicted that church attendance would continue to decline across the next ten years, with only 1.5% believing it would increase. At the very least, this survey shows how demoralising church ministry is for many in the current climate.

However, to borrow from Mark Twain, reports of the death of the Church in the West may be greatly exaggerated. Theologian Harvey Kwiyani points to the vibrant presence of global Christianity in this part of the world.[3] He cites Sheila Akomiah-Conteh's research on church plants in Glasgow, which revealed that over 75% of new churches planted in the city between 2000 and 2015 were African. In London, Kwiyani suggests that 60% of all church attendees are of African descent.

In Peckham, where I've now lived for twenty-five years, you can feel out of place if you're not carrying a Bible on the bus on Sunday morning. Just one mile from my house lies the beginning of the Old Kent Road. On its 1.5 mile stretch you can find over twenty-five Black Majority churches, and there are over two hundred in the surrounding area. If someone were to make a church version of monopoly, how the Old Kent Road's fortunes would change!

Conversely, we must ask, is decline in church attendance necessarily a terrible thing for the spiritual life of a nation? C. S. Lewis, writing on the topic after the Second World War, put it like this:

I am not clear that [religious decline] makes conversion to Christianity rarer or more difficult: rather the reverse. It makes the choice more unescapable. When the Round Table is broken every man must follow either Galahad or Mordred: middle things are gone.[4]

My work at St Mellitus College has brought me into contact with countless people, many under the age of forty, from non-religious, de-churched or other religious backgrounds, who have encountered Christ as adults and are now passionate about sharing the good news with others. As a member of All Saints Peckham these last two and a half decades, I've experienced the church moving from potential closure to being (at one point) the fastest growing Anglican church south of the river. Some of the story of that journey will be told in this book.

Regardless of one's perspective on decline, there is no denying that the world around us is changing. Warning sounds, like that ship's foghorn, can be heard all around us. We are confronted with a new post-Christian world, brimful of challenges to the Church's 'business as usual' but also overflowing with opportunities for people to encounter Christ. And yet, neither the challenges nor the opportunities will be met unless we think critically and creatively about the identity, purpose and mission of the Church. It was Hendrick Kraemer who said, 'the church is always in a state of crisis; and that its greatest shortcoming is that it is only occasionally aware of it'.[5] Maybe our awareness of crisis is our current strength.

The scholar who has most shaped my thinking on the relationship between the Church and the context in which we find ourselves is Lesslie Newbigin. I had the privilege of meeting him when I was in my twenties, and his gentle, humble yet fiercely persuasive approach impacted me as a newbie in the world of theology. Upon returning to the West after decades of overseas missionary work in India, Lesslie Newbigin was struck by the increasingly secular and pluralistic nature of society. He spent his remaining years exploring ways in which the gospel could be made known in the changing culture of Western democracy. One of the conclusions he reached was that traditional rational or apologetic approaches to convincing people of the veracity of the Christian faith would not suffice. Rather, the power of the gospel would be made manifest when lived out within community:

> I have come to feel that the primary reality of which we have to take account in seeking for a Christian impact on public life is the Christian congregation. How is it possible that the gospel should be credible, that people should come to believe that the power which has the last word in human affairs is represented by a man hanging on a cross? I am suggesting that the only answer, the only hermeneutic of the gospel, is a congregation of men and women who believe it and live by it.[6]

It seems that the answer to the decline of the Church in the West lies within the Church and not outside it. What if we met predictions of impending extinction by believing more in its power – the power we as members of the Church have to live out the gospel story as a community together?

It can be easy to view the Church as a retail outlet with a great product we need to market and sell. Or as a social foodbank, providing a service for those in need. Or as a leisure club – a place to connect with other like-minded people and have a great time. The reality is that the Church is the community commissioned by Jesus to live and speak his good news in the world, to be the continuation of his 'good news for everyone' ministry. In the hit BBC programme *Call the Midwife*, the often prophetic and apposite Sister Monica Joan reminds her fellow sisters that God's hands are often present in place of our own and it is God who works through our simple labours of love.

Or to paraphrase Paul McCartney in 'Hey Jude', we have the ability to respond and make things better. We might, it turns out, be the answer to our own problems. Newbigin writes this:

> The work of Jesus is the communication of the name of God to a community. He does not bequeath to posterity a body

of teaching preserved in a book ... He does not leave behind an ideal or a program. He leaves behind a community – the Church.[7]

Ecclesiology is essentially the study of the Church, or rather the theology of the Church, stemming from the most commonly used Greek word to describe the early church gathering (*ekklesia*). The subject of ecclesiology can be rather neglected, but theologian John Stackhouse reveals why it is so relevant and important: 'We need ecclesiology – the doctrine of the church – to clarify our minds, motivate our hearts, and direct our hands. We need ecclesiology so that we can be who and whose we truly are.'[8]

It is crucial, therefore, that we give some thought to the question of ecclesiology in order to understand our identity in challenging and complex times and to know what to do and how to act.

This critical task of discerning whose we are and how we are to be is nothing new. One of the challenges in seeking to write a book about 'the Church' is that we can all too easily talk about it in abstract terms, as if there is some blueprint model of Church to be extracted from the New Testament and applied to ourselves. But the reality is that the Church is always 'in situ', and we can only ever speak of it in a particular time and place.

Paul begins his letter to the Philippians with the following introduction: 'Paul and Timothy, servants of Christ Jesus, to all the saints in Christ Jesus who are in Philippi' (Philippians 1:1). The Philippians are residents of a particular place, and the church in Philippi is finding local expression among real communities, constituted by real people.

However, as the letter develops, Paul writes, 'our citizenship is in heaven, and it is from there that we are expecting a Saviour, the Lord Jesus Christ' (Philippians 3:20). The idea of dual citizenship introduced here is a concept that would have resonated with the Philippian church. Philippi had been the location of a significant Roman battle in which rebel forces against the emperor had been defeated. This meant it was considered a 'colony of Rome' or a 'Rome in miniature', and its people experienced the privileges and rights of Roman citizenship as though they were on Italian soil (despite being over eight hundred miles away). Living in this particular location, subject to the rules and privileges of another more powerful authority, set them apart from other cities in the area.

It is no coincidence then, that Paul adopts this idea of dual citizenship to describe the Christian's identity, expressing as it does something of the tension between present reality and future hope. While those in the Philippian church lived fully as Philippian citizens, they knew that ultimately, they answered to a higher authority; that their 'kingdom in miniature' awaited the return of the king.

In our present day, in whatever location the Church finds itself – whether the wealthy suburbs of the home counties, the inner-city estates of our most urban areas, or the rural villages of the English countryside – the Church is the visible and corporate witness to the new world God is ushering in. Let me explain further.

The book by Newbigin that has most influenced my thinking is *The Household of God*.[9] In this, he coins a wonderful phrase to describe the Church – 'the pilgrim people of God' – which I love because it speaks of our dual identity as the Church of today and the Church of tomorrow. As God's people, we are always to be on the move, never becoming tired and static and stuck in a particular place, but remembering we are on a journey and that our ultimate home is with God in Christ.

I work for the Church of England. It's a vast and influential institution and, despite the aforementioned statistics of decline, it speaks of permanence and stability. While not jettisoning what is good, we can appreciate Newbigin pointing us as a Church to the need to be adaptable and agile, able to respond to the world around us. The analogy he uses is of a pilgrim who has a clear sense of the journey they have embarked on. This is no picture of nomadic wandering; rather, the pilgrim church has its sights set on a future destination, keeping that always in view, aware that it has a foot in two worlds and its life is to point people to Christ. As Newbigin expresses it:

The Church is the pilgrim people of God. It is on the move – hastening to the ends of the earth to beseech all men to be reconciled to God, and hastening to the end of time to meet its Lord who will gather all into one. Therefore, the nature of the Church is never to be finally defined in static terms, but only in terms of that to which it is going. It cannot be understood rightly except in a perspective which is at once missionary and eschatological.[10]

It is in its identity as a pilgrim people that the Church is endowed with the bravery and tenacity to live out the call to be both 'at home' and 'not at home' in the world. We are to have the courage to challenge things that are not as God intends them to be – such as cruelty and injustice – while living in a way that speaks of and points towards God's coming kingdom.

In 2013, the newly elected Pope Francis issued a statement calling for all Christians to see themselves as 'missionary disciples'. This image suggests movement and flexibility, an outward-looking orientation and a commitment to learning together. The pilgrim people of God are a community of missionary disciples, and *Living His Story Together* is my contribution to the ongoing conversation about what this means in the world today. My intention has been to write a love letter to the Church, not chastising us to pull up our socks and do better but reminding us of the privilege to which we have been called. The fact that God has entrusted the living out of the gospel of Jesus to people like you and me is both humbling and challenging.

Each of the six chapters that follows takes a different theme on what it is to be a community of missionary disciples. First, I seek to offer some engagement with Scripture and current theological thinking on the nature and identity of the Church, before offering four principles for practice. These aren't intended to be prescriptive or the definitive word on how the Church should 'direct her hands'. Rather, they seek to offer threads of wisdom that might cause you to think about how we can face the challenges and opportunities that this current moment brings. My hope is that these threads may be woven together to create something colourful and beautiful. You will also find questions to think about personally or discuss in small groups within your church.

As I write, war is raging in Israel and Palestine and Ukraine, and we are on the cusp of a global refugee crisis hitherto unknown. Christians in Manipur and other parts of the world are being brutally persecuted. Closer to home, people face a cost-of-living crisis. Poverty is on the increase as more and more families find themselves on the breadline, unable to feed their children and heat their homes. Politically, we seem more divided than ever, and systemic racism and sexual abuse is being uncovered in some of our most influential institutions, including the Church. It can feel overwhelming. How are we to respond? Do we speak up or carry on serving quietly, trying to make a difference within our local communities? Should we fear the worst? Are the prospects for the Church good or bad? Newbigin expresses this predicament well: 'I am neither an optimist nor a pessimist. Jesus Christ is risen from the dead.'[11]

The promise of Jesus that he would build his Church and nothing would stand against it (Matthew 16:18) seems more powerful and necessary than ever before. As God's missionary disciples, we are the ones called to live out the gospel story of the risen Jesus in times of challenge and turmoil, looking for signs of new life and growth that only God's Spirit can bring. My hope and prayer is that this book would be an encouragement to us as we seek to do that together.

1

Church and mission: Does the Church have a mission?

The Church exists by mission just as a fire exists by burning. Where there is no mission there is no Church.[1]

When my son Asher was three years old, we visited a friend's church one Sunday morning for a christening service. The church we were part of as a family was very informal with a worship band – this much more traditional one had a robed choir and organ. As we sat in silence at the start of the service, I closed my eyes to pray. I was enjoying the peaceful presence of God, when suddenly there came the loud voice of my toddler asking, 'Mummy, where's the drum kit?' It seems that from an early age we can hold certain assumptions about what church is like and what should and shouldn't be part of it.

The question, 'What is the identity and purpose of the Church?' is a complex one on which many books have already been written. The fiery statement from the Swiss Theologian Emil Brunner that opens this chapter suggests that the Church can only understand itself in relation to its mission; mission is core to the identity of the Church; mission is the essence (whether you have a drum kit or an organ or even both!). This sentiment has been reaffirmed more recently through the increasingly popular phrase 'missional church', which seems to have become common parlance in some spheres and so overused in others that it has potentially lost the edge of its intended meaning.[2]

What are we to make of missional church? One of the instigators of the phrase is a theologian called Darrell Guder who wrote a book with that title in the 1990s.[3] Guder suggests that the word 'missional' is a form of scaffolding, holding up our theology and understanding of Church. In one sense, we shouldn't really need it, but until we see ourselves fundamentally rooted in our identity as God's missionary disciples, we need the phrase to help keep us on track. In his subsequent book *Called To Witness*, Guder says this: 'If mission were truly the mother of our theology, if our theological disciplines were intentionally conceived and developed as components of the formation of the church for its biblical vocation, we would never need to use the term "missional".'[4]

It seems then that the inclusion of the word 'missional' is to remind the Church of its primary vocation and identity – a kind of clarion call, rousing it from its comfortable slumber. However, the use of the phrase 'missional' as a descriptor for church is also associated with the Western Church's needs to understand itself as now operating within a post-Christendom climate and its desire to rethink the term 'mission' itself.

Mission in a post-Christendom world

During the Christendom era – from the mid-fourth century to the mid-twentieth century – the Church in the West held a dominant position within society. However, as secularisation swept through the West, it began to find itself in the minority, frequently at odds with culture's values and priorities. In a post-Christendom climate, the Christian narrative is no longer an important part of our corporate memory. Few people even know the Christian story, let alone look to it as a governing narrative for their lives.

This was brought home to me recently when a non-church friend told me that her four-year-old daughter had picked up a Christmas card posted through the letter box. Pointing at the stamp, she asked her mum who was in the picture. 'That's baby Jesus and Mary.' The girl replied incredulously, 'Jesus? What's he got to do with Christmas?'

In Easter 2022, one of the UK's mainstream supermarkets advertised a range of gins with the strapline, 'Make Good

Friday Great'. Such sentiments could only be offered in a post-Christendom world. While some of us mourn the loss of faith's centrality in our culture, others are excited by the possibility of forging a new sense of identity. After all, the early church was a movement of missionary disciples living within a pluralistic and changing culture, a prophetic minority. The phrase 'missional church' acknowledges our shift in social status and position, and we may well welcome the opportunity to reimagine and reidentify with the Church's original calling and purpose.

However, it must also be acknowledged that the shift to a post-Christendom and post-colonial culture means that the term 'mission' itself may also be problematic – and putting an 'al' on the end of the word can't disguise that. While there were, of course, many missionaries who sacrificially loved and served others in the name of Christ during the Christendom era, there is, lamentably, an expression of mission which has colluded with colonialism and has been carried out in a spirit of conquest and domination, at times even complicit in some of the most horrendous crimes of the era. For many in our communities, the word 'mission' evokes a reaction of discomfort or even pain.

In the summer of 2021, I had the privilege of attending a Zoom call with some Anglican clergy in the Canadian province of Quebec. They had read *Living His Story* and wished to discuss it with me during a study day on faith-sharing. These clergy were spread far and wide over some of the most remote parts of the province, and several of them were First Nation Christian believers who had followed a vocation to Christian ministry.

Two weeks before the planned Zoom call, the media reported the discovery of the unmarked graves of 215 children at the Kamloops Indian Residential School in British Columbia, which had closed in 1978. Such schools operated during the nineteenth and twentieth centuries as a joint venture between the government and the religious authorities in an attempt to assimilate the indigenous children. That anything so shocking or terrible could happen in the first place is horrific, while the idea of the Church being associated leaves one cold. Over subsequent weeks, as further unmarked graves were found and stories of grief and tragedy told, Canadian Prime minister Justin Trudeau spoke of a 'painful reminder' of 'a shameful chapter of our country's history'.[5]

The latest revelations, so close to my appointment with the clergy, made me anxious. How could I talk about mission and evangelism in this context? I sought the advice of the kind priest who had invited me, and suggested instead that we spent the time sharing stories and simply talking and praying together. Eventually the day came, and it is hard to express how a Zoom meeting could feel so much like holy ground, so much like a space full of the presence of God. I was honoured to share the story of how Jesus had changed my life but, more importantly, I was both privileged and heartbroken to share with those who had witnessed first-hand the atrocities, to hear their anger and grief, and yet also to witness their love for Christ and the communities they served. It was a humbling experience that I doubt I will ever forget.

And so, as I come to reflect on the topic of 'mission', with my dear Canadian brothers and sisters in mind, I can't help but be aware of the connotations and distrust the terms brings. It is fair to say that there has been a justifiable crisis in confidence with regard to the use of the words 'mission' and 'missionary'. Brian McLaren, one of the leading figures in the emerging church movement in the United States, suggests we suffer from 'post-colonial embarrassment with the term missionary'.[6] For those of us who feel positive about the word 'mission' and presume it is always motivated by love and service, it is important to sit and hear the stories of those who perceive it differently and to understand the centuries of pain and hurt with which the word can be associated.

Less painful, but equally problematic, is that mission can also have connotations of a success- or numbers-oriented approach. Mission plans and strategy may become unhelpfully caught up with targets and counting bums on seats (or pews, depending on your ecclesiastical preference!). Those seeking to pioneer creative mission initiatives can face the pressure of having to prove their effectiveness in order to secure financial support, and effectiveness nearly always equals numbers in attendance.

So, should we abandon the term? If mission runs the risk of being associated with the very worst incarnation of its practice, perhaps it would be better to desist from using the word completely and come up with an alternative? In order to address this, let's explore what the term 'mission' means in the first place.

Defining mission

The word occurs sparingly in the English translation of the Bible. It stems from the Latin verb *mitto* (with *missio* being the noun form) and simply means 'to send'. *Mitto* is a translation of the Greek verb *apostello* which occurs over 130 times in the New Testament and means 'to send' or 'to send out'. It is also the linguistic origin of the term 'apostle'.

Mission as sending

In the New Testament, there are three great sendings which are connected with the good news of the gospel. The first is the sending by the Father of his Son Jesus into the world. In the heart-warming gospel story where Jesus welcomes the children, he describes his Father as 'the one who sent me' (Luke 9:48). This is just one of over forty references in the New Testament to Jesus as the 'sent one'. Jesus is the one 'missioned' into the world to do the will of the Father – this special mission finding its origin in the saving and redeeming love of God for the world (John 3:16–17).

The second sending in the New Testament is the sending of the Spirit. When faced with the anxiety of the disciples who have recently learned of his impending departure, Jesus informs them that another like him is coming. Jesus is, of course, talking about the Holy Spirit, who is described in John's Gospel as the Advocate or Helper, and is spoken of as the one who will 'remind you of all that I have said to you' (John 14:26). There is a clear connection here between the sending of the Son and the later sending of the Spirit who will both remind the disciples of the things Jesus said and help them, in turn, to know what to say when they are standing before opposing authorities (Luke 12:12). This foretelling of the Spirit in John's farewell discourse is dramatically realised at the beginning of the book of Acts on the day of Pentecost, when the disciples, gathered together in one place, receive the Spirit through signs and wonders.

The third sending in the New Testament is the sending of the church into the world by Jesus himself: 'As you have sent me into the world, so I have sent them into the world' (John 17:18).

It seems from this verse that the Church's sending into the world is to be like that of Jesus, and it is within this context that Jesus goes on to pray for the unity of the Church as a demonstration and manifestation of his own sending. It is through the sent-out and lived-out life of the Church that the world is to believe Jesus himself is sent by God.

These three acts of sending come together in some of the last words Jesus spoke to his disciples. On one of the occasions when the risen Jesus meets with the disciples, he says to them, "'Peace be with you. As the Father has sent me, so I send you." When he had said this, he breathed on them and said to them, "Receive the Holy Spirit"' (John 20:21–2).

Jesus speaks of himself as the one who has been sent by God and so now sends his disciples in the same way. This is the last of the forty times that Jesus is spoken of as the one who is sent. He now becomes also the one who sends. The giving of the Holy Spirit is clearly connected to the sending of the first disciples in this way.

Missionary disciples

As the New Testament describes it, mission it is less about a particular activity and more about a direction or orientation; less about a strategy and more about receiving a divine gift; less about targets and numbers and more about an outward-looking posture towards the world. From its very beginning, the Church was to understand itself as missionary (sent) disciples who were sent by the one who himself was sent, as those who receive the sending of the Spirit to equip them for this calling. It is hard to see how this identity and calling can have anything to do with oppression, subjugation and coercion. If mission has come to signify those things to people, instead of this original intention of a movement or orientation of divine love, then there is certainly a good argument for doing away with the word entirely.

However, it is also the case that the word 'disciple' no longer seems to convey this outward posture. It has become commonly associated with more internal aspects of discipleship, such as studying the Bible, prayer and drawing closer to God. My fear is that if we were to drop the word 'mission' entirely, we might lose the idea of 'sentness' that is originally intended in the Gospels. I am reminded of Barth's famous chide that theology which has forgotten mission is 'pious and sacred egocentricity'.[7] What we need is not a new word but a better way of expressing our mission, which demonstrates that hard and painful lessons have been learned from the misappropriation of this concept, and that mission itself needs to be realigned with these three sendings. It is crucial we imagine mission as not merely action in response to the good news of the kingdom, but active participation within it, characterised by humility and repentance. Missional, then, is a way of viewing mission not so much as an activity of the Church but as an outward-looking posture:

> Mission is not just a program of the church. It defines the church as God's sent people. Either we are defined by mission, or we reduce the scope of the gospel and the mandate of the church. Thus our challenge today is to move from church with mission to missional church.[8]

My hope and prayer for the remainder of this book is that it would help us imagine mission in a way that reflects this orientation of sentness, rather than a preoccupation with numbers and success, and is far removed from notions of coercion, subjugation and oppression.

Is everyone a missionary?

Before moving on, there is one final reflection to make. When talking about mission as 'sending', it is natural to think of missionaries who are sent overseas, thousands of miles from where they grew up. I have a friend who is a missionary in Chile, and I enjoy reading her prayer letter updates of the ministry she is involved in – it is cross-cultural in every sense of the word. However, if mission is just about the calling of the gifted and courageous few, the Church which remains is, by definition, not sent but the one who sends. John 20:21, though, makes clear that all the disciples are sent, not only particular few, but each and every one of them. The posture of sentness is to define the whole Church.

As a sent community, there will be particular callings and vocations for all, different ways of living out our corporate sentness. Some will carry out their calling to be a sent people by moving to other places to love and serve there. Others will carry out their calling to be a sent people by serving in business, healthcare, education, in the home and among children. Others will carry out their calling to be a sent people through giving their time fully to the ministry of the Church. Others will carry out their calling as a sent people by moving to the West from global parts of the Church that are thriving, bringing new enthusiasm and vigour to our faith. The truth is we are all sent. We are all the ones to whom the one who himself was sent now gives his Spirit. We are all missionary disciples of the Sent One.

This raises the question: has the Church always seen itself that way, or is this is a new idea based on the needs of a Church in decline? Let's look further back than the New Testament and explore how the Old Testament views the idea of God's gathered community.

A missional way of reading Scripture

We call this way of reading Scripture a missional hermeneutic. We're regarding the Bible as a record of the actions and interventions of a missionary God into the world he created, looking at salvation history across time, through different people and in different contexts, until it reaches its climax in the life, death and resurrection of Jesus and the sending of the Spirit. Reading Scripture this way is rather like putting on special glasses when you have the option of viewing a film in 3D. You don't simply see the events narrated before you, you get caught up in the drama too. The first 3D movie I ever experienced was a nature film set in the deep ocean. It was like swimming in the sea myself, surrounded by brightly coloured fish, and there was a moment when I flinched, feeling a shark was brushing right past!

Putting on 3D missional glasses when reading the Bible is a bit like this. It is to discover ourselves as part of the action, immersed deeply within the narrative of God who loves and sends and saves. If you watch a 3D movie without special glasses, you can follow the plot without a problem – it's just a little fuzzy. But you miss out on so much! Putting on 3D missional glasses means we are not observers by the side of the road, watching the action pass us by. We're not merely impassive readers of a story that happened to others and not to us. A missional hermeneutic draws us into God's story and compels us to ask the question, 'Who am I?' and, perhaps more importantly, 'Who are we?' As we explore the action and intervention of God in different times and contexts, and among different people groups and nations, we're compelled to think of our own contexts – as different as they may be – and to ask, 'What is God doing in this time and in this place?

Chris Wright, one of the primary scholars offering such an approach to reading the Bible, said this about how it impacts our behaviour and action: 'Fundamentally, our mission (if it is biblically informed and validated) means our committed participation as God's people, at God's invitation and command, in God's own mission within the history of the world for the redemption of God's creation.'[9]

A missionary reading of Scripture also drives us out from our safe and comfortable spaces to engage with those around us. The famous missiologist Harvie Conn described the task of the missiologist as being that of interrupting theological conversations with the words 'among the nations', provoking us to look outwards and beyond ourselves. We're nudged to see the unexpected, to look at what God is doing among unlikely people, in forgotten and neglected places. The persistent refrain 'among the nations' means we cannot seek refuge in the comfort of nationalism which numbs us to the needs of the rest of the world. Our gaze must be directed outwards and beyond to see unpredictable and sometimes hidden things. Reflecting on the ways in which God acted and intervened in other times and in other places enables us to consider our own moment. It compels us gaze upon the margins, the outsiders, the unexpected places where we find God at work, and in so doing, forces us to question our own privilege and use of power in contemporary church activity and in many of our current missionary practices.

Alongside the questions 'Who am I?' and 'What is God doing in this time and this place?', a missionary reading of Scripture leads us to ask, 'What does it mean to be God's missionary disciples in the world today? How can we play our part?'

The place it all begins – the Old Testament

It could be argued that if one is truly to explore a missional reading of Scripture, one must start right at the very beginning, with the origins of human life itself in the book of Genesis. While there is much that we must draw from the creation account as we think about being missionary disciples – not least the recognition that each and every person we encounter is created and loved by God – our exploration will commence a little further on. My interest is to discern what themes are paramount in the notion of 'community', and the account of Abraham's call and his covenant with God seems a good place to begin. In due course, we'll draw four principles for practice from this.

Abraham – the first missionary disciple?

The story of Abraham begins in Ur, a great city of the ancient world, in what would now be southern Iraq. Ur was a busy and thriving centre and today you can still see the remains of a ziggurat (a tower like the tower of Babel) devoted to the god Nanna, one of the many gods of the Mesopotamian pantheon. If one thing has been made clear in the opening eleven chapters of the Bible, it is humankind's propensity to make a mess of things, to wander away, to hurt, to kill and essentially to mar the image of God within us. Here, however, the focus homes in on one individual through whom God intends to bring about a universal blessing – a man named Abram (later to be called Abraham, meaning 'Father of Nations'). Against the backdrop of a creation out of kilter and a humanity at enmity with its fellow inhabitants, God remarkably chooses an older couple with fertility problems as the starting point of a new community. The call of Abraham is connected with the nation of Israel, yet we are also invited to see the cosmic significance of these two individuals. Through one earthly couple, the human race which has turned in on itself, will be reset. As Walter Brueggemann says:

> the purpose of the call is to fashion an alternative community in creation gone awry, to embody in human history the power of the blessing. It is the hope of God that in this new family all human history can be brought to the unity and harmony intended by the one who calls.[10]

So, Abraham is chosen, out of all the citizens of Ur, to be the one through whom God will do a new thing, the one through whom God will reset and draw back his beloved creation. These verses at the beginning of Genesis 12 are crucial for understanding the nature and purpose of his calling:

> I will make you into a great nation,
>   and I will bless you;
> I will make your name great,
>   and you will be a blessing.
> I will bless those who bless you,
>   and whoever curses you I will curse;
> and all peoples on earth
>   will be blessed through you.
> (Genesis 12:2–3, NIVUK)

The promise is that through this ageing pair, a great nation will follow that will flourish and prosper. It is striking that in contrast to the architects of the tower of Babel (Genesis 11:4), who sought to make a name for themselves, God is the one here promising to make Abraham's name great. Most importantly, God's promise is universal in scope – it encompasses not only Abraham's family and his descendants, not only his fellow residents of Ur, but all people. It is hard to read this passage without thinking forward to verses in the New Testament which echo the idea of the blessing of all nations. We can hardly fail to note that Matthew chooses to begin his gospel with Abraham – noting him as the first forefather in the genealogy which leads to Jesus – and to end his account with the famous words known as the Great Commission, in which the disciples are sent to make disciples of 'all nations'.

Four principles for practice

Let's consider four principles for practice that we can draw from Abraham's story.

1 Mission starts and ends with God

To begin with, we're reminded of that most cherished of all principles – that God is a missionary God. Scholars use the Latin phrase *missio Dei* to express the conviction that mission is not an activity of the Church first and foremost, but finds its origin in the character and being of God. This idea was first articulated by Karl Barth at a missionary conference in the 1930s (then later developed by Hartenstein and others at a further conference in Willengen in 1952) to demonstrate that the missionary initiative lies not with the Church as the one who sends missionaries into the world, but in the God who is himself a missionary. God calls Abraham to leave Ur because God is the living Lord, the Creator and Saviour of the whole world – not of just one particular tribe or people group.

Scholars have expressed the idea of God's missionary nature in a number of different ways. Stephen Holmes suggests that mission can be seen as a divine attribute, just as we might talk about God's love or his faithfulness. Holmes regards God's 'sending' as an eternally purposeful movement of generosity, directed towards God's creation. Scholar John Flett views things slightly differently and suggests that mission isn't an attribute of God on a par with patience or kindness, but rather intrinsic to God's eternal decision to be for humanity. He sees all God's attributes as having a missionary purpose because they are directed towards the world God has made. I've found this idea a helpful and moving one, especially when I've been meeting or speaking with people in times of trouble or suffering. Knowing that God has decided to be eternally for his world gives us hope and enables us to draw comfort from his love.

I'm reminded of the story Jesus tells of the two sons. One prematurely wrests his inheritance from his family, cuts off all ties and squanders his newfound wealth in hedonistic pursuit. Desperate and out of options he reluctantly returns home, fearing the judgement and chastisement of his father. His father, however, is out looking for him; in fact, he has never stopped looking for his son since the day he left. Glimpsing the young man in the distance, he picks up his robes and, in a manner undignified for a middle Eastern man of his status, runs to embrace his son and celebrate his beloved's return. It is the most powerful picture of a God who has eternally decided to be *for* his creation.

Mission is not our idea and it will not be our clever strategies that triumph, for mission finds its origin, energy and strength in the divine mission of God, and also its manner and pattern. The way of our missionary God is not triumphalistic or coercive, but humble and gentle. A baby is born in obscurity to a teenage girl without fanfare or wealth... our mission as the Church today must take heed of that and nothing else.

A beautiful episode of *Call the Midwife* expresses this sentiment. Pupil Nurse Corrigan is being scolded for keeping secret the fact that she had a daughter born outside of marriage. In the midst of a barrage of chastisement, the elderly, sagacious Sister Monica Joan cuts through with the striking insight that if Corrigan's actions have cast her out to the edges of society, then the edges are where the nuns should minister and work.

Wherever the missional God is present and wherever those who need to know the compassion of God reside, that is where the missional church must be found.

2 Mission involves the particular and the universal

Through the story of Abraham, we are introduced to the concepts of universality and particularity, and the way in which these weave together throughout the biblical narrative. At the very beginning of the Bible, we see God as a universal God – the God who creates the heavens and the earth. God is the Creator and Sustainer of all. However, in the story of Abraham, we are introduced to a particular family of people, and it is through this particular people that the purposes of the universal God are carried out. It is not that the focus switches from the universal to the particular but that the two intertwine. The end goal is not the city of Ur, not even the great city of Jerusalem, but the universal city of God – the new Jerusalem – of Revelation 21:2. The writer of the book of Hebrews notes that this universal goal beyond his own time and moment was the focus of Abraham's hope, 'For he looked forward to the city that has foundations, whose architect and builder is God' (Hebrews 11:10).

Out of all the possible inhabitants of the city of Ur, God's focus narrows in on one couple – Abraham and Sarah. This idea of God choosing a particular family or individual can seem problematic and raises the difficult question, 'Does God have favourites?' I remember once being introduced to a man who was accompanied by his four children. He presented them to me in turn, and as he came to his last son, he said, 'This is Thomas, he's my favourite'. I laughed, assuming this must be a joke, but the man was deadly serious and a rather awkward atmosphere lingered. Despite the frequency with which I am asked by my own three sons, I refuse to entertain even the possibility of having a favourite. I love them all (and am exasperated by them) in equal measure. And surely the idea of a God having favourites – though maybe we're sometimes tempted to think that his love is only for a few, the special ones who make the grade – contradicts the notion of *missio Dei*? As we

22

explore the story of Abraham, we see that those who receive God's blessing are also those who are to give it. There is a reciprocity at work here that must lie at the heart of all our explorations of mission – to receive blessing is to give blessing. Abraham's family is chosen to be the particular one through whom God would bless the universal family of the world. Abraham is only God's favourite in order to demonstrate that all God's children are his favourites.

When I was a student worker, I used to see Eleanor every week for a Bible study. She had not been raised in a Christian family but had met Christians at university who had introduced her to Jesus, and he was slowly and wonderfully transforming her. We would meet in the cafeteria at Goldsmiths University to read and discuss the Bible together, which was an entirely new experience for her. Having been brought up with very little knowledge of Jesus' life, she had loved discovering his healings and parables in Mark's Gospel.

One week, we were planning on looking at the beginning of Ephesians together. I was a bit apprehensive, wondering what she might make of some of the opening chapter, which talks about God's election and choice. We took time to read silently through the opening verses of the letter, and as she came to the phrase, 'he chose us in Christ before the foundation of the world', Eleanor asked, 'Does this mean God chooses people?' She immediately looked down at the Bible again and, in the silence, I noticed tears welling up and dropping down onto its pages. Then she said, 'I just can't believe God would choose me.'

God's spotlight on particular people in particular times and places is never a cause for pride or self-congratulation, as if something about us makes us exceptionally worthy or useful to God. God can reveal his love quite well without us, but he chooses to use us in our particular circumstances to be the ones through whom he blesses others. As Eleanor was discovering in that moment, God had reached out and shown his love to her, and through her was going to show his love to others. Chris Wright says we need to start seeing the concept of election as a 'doctrine of mission' and not 'a calculus for the arithmetic of salvation'.[11] As Abraham's story demonstrates, the goal of a particular people receiving God's blessing was so that 'all peoples' might in turn be blessed. This Abrahamic promise of the blessing of 'all peoples' is repeated five times throughout Genesis (12:3, 18:18, 22:18, 26:4 and 28:14). With the hindsight provided by the New Testament, our focus is drawn to the similar phrase used repeatedly in the book of Revelation, both in 7:9 and 22:2, when all nations gather around the throne of the Lamb, and where the leaves of the trees in the heavenly city are for the healing of the nations. In the missional economy of God, the particular is the vehicle through which the universal is blessed. And so, lest we get too caught up in a vision of end-time glory, this principle of the particular and the universal causes us to ask, who might be those 'all peoples' we could be a blessing to? Who are the 'all nations' situated in and around our particular churches that we are being encouraged to have in view, to pray for and to seek to be a blessing to? As Abraham shows us, one of the most crucial foundations of all mission is the recognition that those who have received blessing from God are to be blessings to others. Mission is ultimately rooted in generosity.

3 Mission is about blessing as well as saving

When it comes to mission activities in the Church, we can have a tendency to launch into 'action mode', not always taking time to stop and ask why we're doing certain things. Our default position may be that of problem fixer: we know the world's a mess and we want to make a difference. Perhaps we even articulate this as wanting to 'save' people. Of course, the notion of salvation lies at the heart of Scripture and at the centre of the gospel message we seek to share. As Peter announced to the crowd gathered at Pentecost, 'everyone who calls on the name of the Lord will be saved' (Acts 2:21). But what does it mean to be 'saved'? Depending on our background, we may have a fairly limited idea of what this is about, possibly around praying the sinner's prayer, or starting to attend church. However, Abraham's missionary mandate is framed in much more expansive and global terms. The goal is not recruitment; he is not to build an empire but rather to bless the world: 'all peoples on earth will be blessed through you' (Genesis 12:3, NIVUK).

God's goal for human life is for it to flourish. One of the TV programmes that has steadily crept up the UK ratings list in recent years is the BBC's *The Repair Shop*. It is known to stir strong emotions in even the hardest of hearts! Hosted by the charming Jay Blades, a former furniture restorer himself, *The Repair Shop* focuses each week on a number of individuals who have a family heirloom, which is either broken or in a state of disrepair. Through the meticulous hard work of skilled professionals, objects which were damaged, or simply lying around gathering dust, are tenderly restored to their former glory (indeed, some end up looking even more beautiful than they did originally), and when brought back to life, used for a new purpose.

In one recent episode, a man named Nick and his granddaughter brought in a violin that was over a hundred years old. It was in a terrible state, scratched and broken and lacking strings. Many years earlier, it had been played in various jazz bands by Nick's grandfather, who had emigrated from the Bahamas in the 1920s. Although Nick had only met his grandfather a couple of times, when he was still a child, a love of music had been passed through the generations, and Nick longed for the dusty violin to be used for its true purpose once again. It was quite a task for the violin restorer – she had rarely seen a violin in worse condition than this but gladly rose to the challenge. Over a period of weeks, through much blood, sweat and tears, the violin was completely repaired. Watching Nick hold it in his hand, lift it to his chin and play was a beautiful TV moment.

The image of restoration is a helpful one to have in mind as we think about salvation in mission. Through Abraham, God is beginning his reset programme. The creation that was meant to be in harmony with God and with itself is in a state of discord. However, God will not leave things as they are, and through Abraham he begins his process of restoring the world to its original purpose. As we journey through Scripture, it is clear that the focus of this restoration is the sending and saving work of his only son, Jesus. As Chris Wright writes so eloquently, 'The Mission of God is to redeem the whole of creation, broken by sin and evil, into the new creation, populated by the redeemed from every culture, through the cross and resurrection of Christ.'[12]

In this scheme, mission isn't just about saving people; it isn't just about recruitment or problem fixing. It's ultimately about the flourishing of the world – God's creation – and those who live in it being restored to their intended purpose. This way of looking at mission, as being about flourishing and blessing rather than projects (however well-meant or worthy), can expand our vision of what we are called to in our local communities. It means that acts of service, caring for creation and witnessing in words are all part of what it means to be a missionary disciple.

4 Mission involves community

It is through a community that God chooses to bring about his reset and blessing. Mission and community, therefore, go hand in hand and we see this clearly in Acts, in the first gatherings of the disciples after Pentecost. As the disciples met together, praying, breaking bread and reading the Scriptures, they 'had all things in common: they would sell their possessions and goods and distribute the proceeds to all, as any had need' (Acts 2:44–5). Even at this early stage, before Paul even comes onto the scene, the disciples knew that God's blessing was not for personal fulfilment but was intended rather to overflow outwards to those in need. There is a community shape to post-Pentecost faith. As Guder writes:

> Mission is not just a program of the church. It defines the church as God's sent people. Either we are defined by mission, or we reduce the scope of the gospel and the mandate of the church. Thus our challenge today is to move from church with mission to missional church.[13]

Mission and community

And so, it's worth taking some time near the beginning of this book to reflect on our own experiences and involvement with church. To what extent does your church regard itself as a missionary community? Is mission seen more as something for those who are particularly keen and called? How might reimagining ourselves as God's missionary people affect the way we think about everything we do at church, from Sunday services, to our work with young people, to our lives outside of the church's walls? These are vital questions to address if we are to live the story of Jesus together in our communities.

Let's draw again on Abraham's story as we think about this connection between mission and community. As the story unfolds through the pages of Genesis, Abraham's wife Sarah does indeed, against all odds, bear a son named Isaac, who in turn is father to Jacob, who in turn is father to twelve sons. Gradually, the family of many which God told Abraham about moves from the abstract into reality. God has carved himself out a people who are on a journey towards the promised land.

But how does this new family line become a blessing to the rest of the world? It is arguable that all Abraham and Sarah experience of God's promise being fulfilled concerns their miraculous conception of a child and their willingness to dwell in tents so they could move at any time. As the writer to the Hebrews reminds us, Abraham looked forward to that which he could not see. There are, in fact, three distinctives of the community which enacts God's blessing to the world:

1 A community of righteousness and justice

We first hear of Sodom in Genesis 13:12, and it is later described as a city of 'grave sin'. Sodom depicts in microcosm the fallenness which the first twelve chapters of Genesis have described. While Abraham and his descendants are promised blessing, Sodom will face the judgement of God. In the midst of one of the most interesting conversations in the Bible, when God and Abraham debate how many righteous people there would need to be in Sodom to hold off God's judgement, we are given an insight into how Abraham and his family will be a blessing to the world – even to places like Sodom and Gomorrah: 'I have chosen him, that he may charge his children and his household after him to keep the way of the LORD by doing righteousness and justice' (Genesis 18:19).

God's people are going to be a blessing because, in contrast to the way of oppression and suffering caused by the actions of Sodom and Gomorrah, they are going to keep the way of the Lord by pursuing righteousness and holiness. In other words, Abraham's people are to be different: their distinctiveness is not purely of a religious nature (for example, in the way they worship), but also has a social dimension. When reflecting on mission, it is easy to get caught up in dualistic thinking. Perhaps we feel social action and evangelism are at odds with each other. Perhaps we fear that if some event or activity doesn't directly proclaim the gospel, then it isn't distinctively Christian. Conversely, we may worry that if evangelism is always tagged onto social action, it can be seen as manipulative and disingenuous. We'll consider this further later in the book. For now, it's sufficient to note that God's people are called to be distinctive and known as his own, and integral to this is pursuing righteousness (living the right way) and justice (putting right that which is wrong). If mission finds its origin in the being and character of God, then any mission activity which flows from the God who loves justice, who hears the voices of the oppressed and responds to their calls, must have this social dimension at its heart.

2 A community of worship and presence

Our default way of thinking can be to associate mission with activity and busyness. In moments of global crisis, the Church often rightly responds with direct action, rushing to provide aid. In the early stages of the first Covid lockdown in spring 2020, as elderly people were isolated in their homes, it was often the local church, alongside other charitable agencies, that leapt into action, arranging meals on wheels, shopping rotas and food parcels for those unable or too vulnerable to make it to the shops. Mission as action certainly has its place.

However, when we consider the people of God in the Old Testament, we find the emphasis is not always on action and activity. Busyness does not seem to be the badge of faithfulness to God. I have to confess that as a child, I was not a very good

Brownie. The Brownie Law never really caught my imagination, and in contrast to the girls who appeared to achieve a new badge each week – proudly sewing an increasingly long display of badges down the arm of their uniforms – I seem to remember I only managed one badge before I left (for making a cup of tea of all things!) While busyness and action can be a part of mission, too much emphasis on these things can involve losing focus on other important aspects.

Returning to the Old Testament, what we see as God's people, embarking on their great journey is a community formed, not primarily around activity, but around covenantal relationship and worship. Writer Jamie Smith says this:

> We become what we worship because what we worship is what we love … It's not a question of whether you worship, but what you worship … To be human is to be a liturgical animal, a creature whose loves are shaped by worship. And worship isn't optional.[14]

Worship is not the antithesis of mission or a rival priority in the Church: worship is what orients us to love God and therefore be the 'aroma of Christ' (2 Corinthians 2:15) in the world today. Newbigin points us towards the fact that in the worship and sacramental life of the church, God's new society is shaped and formed:

> The local Christian congregation, where the word of the gospel is preached, where in the sacrament of the Eucharist we are united with Christ in his dying for the sin of the world and in his risen life for the sake of the world, is the place where we are enabled to develop a shared life in which sin can be both recognised and forgiven. If this congregation understands its true character as a holy priesthood for the sake of the world, and if its members are equipped for the exercise of that priesthood in their secular employments, then there is a point of growth for a new social order.[15]

3 A community of representation

Who Do You Think You Are? is a BAFTA award-winning programme that first aired in 2004. In each episode, a celebrity traces their genealogy. The revelations are sometimes amusing, often enlightening and occasionally devastating, as those taking part learn, for example, of past tragedies, or hidden crimes or extraordinary ancestors they would never have dreamt of having! We are drawn to these discoveries because we are a story people, and knowing where we came from and what has shaped our family's past helps us to understand who we are here and now.

The people of Israel were people with a story – indeed, a truly remarkable story that is probably familiar to most of us. Long after Abraham, Isaac and Jacob, God's people were enduring a miserable existence under oppression in Egypt, forced to work as slaves making bricks out of straw. In the midst of their suffering, God heard their cries, and through the unexpected leadership of Moses, staged a spectacular rescue (involving a catalogue of plagues, famine and the miraculous crossing of the Red Sea). For any Jew after this time, their answer to the question 'Who do you think you are?' would be, 'a people set free by God'. This story would be passed on down the generations, rehearsed from old to young.

> You have seen what I did to the Egyptians, and how I bore you on eagles' wings and brought you to myself. Now therefore, if you obey my voice and keep my covenant, you shall be my treasured possession out of all the peoples. Indeed, the whole earth is mine, but you shall be for me a priestly kingdom and a holy nation. These are the words that you shall speak to the Israelites.
> (Exodus 19:4–6)

We should note that while Israel has a special relationship with God – he calls them 'his treasured possession' – he then reminds them that 'the whole earth is mine'. In the midst of their call to be a holy nation and a priestly kingdom, they must not forget that God is the Creator and Lord of all nations, the God of all peoples. In fact, that understanding would be integral to how they were to live out their priestly role. For the way Israel was to be a blessing to the rest of the world (as promised in Genesis 12:3) was through fulfilling its priestly function. The priestly role is one of representation. The people of Israel were to represent God to the people around them. They were to do this through the way they lived, by pursuing holiness and distinctive living, through the pursuit of justice and righteousness, and through telling the story of God.

This idea is one that Paul picks up in the New Testament. In speaking to the Corinthian church he says, 'we are ambassadors for Christ, since God is making his appeal through us, we entreat you on behalf of Christ, be reconciled to God' (2 Corinthians 5:20). Paul saw his role as a missionary disciple to be one of representation; he was to serve on behalf of God. An ambassador is someone who represents the interests of a particular country or state to others. They often live away from home and are there to speak and act on behalf of their government.

I once attended the open day of a south London secondary school where the head teacher talked about the importance of school uniform. He reminded the boys that as long as they were wearing their uniform, they were representing the school, and cautioned them against anti-social behaviour which would bring the school into disrepute. The implication was, 'If you want to mess around then do it wearing your own clothes!' However, being an ambassador for Christ does not involve having a uniform we can slip in and out of. It concerns our whole lives. Our character, our actions and our words should all point to the reality of a living and loving God. My friend Sarah recently received the utmost compliment from a friend of hers: 'The way you live your life makes me believe there is a God.'

As the Church, our role is to tell the story of God – the story God is writing in each of our lives – to the world. This connects clearly with the idea of witnesses in the New Testament, a term not connected with professional activity, but used to describe ordinary followers of Jesus who simply speak of the extraordinary love of God. Newbigin puts it like this:

> The business of the church is to tell and embody a story, the story of God's mighty acts in creation and redemption and of God's promises concerning what will be in the end. The church affirms the truth of this story by celebrating it, interpreting it and enacting it in the life of the contemporary world. It has no other way of affirming its truth … The church's affirmation is that the story that it tells, embodies and enacts is the true story and that others are to be evaluated by reference to it.[16]

The question we have to ask ourselves is this: how good have we been at telling the story of God and passing on this message? How good have we been at embodying the story of God's redemption and restoration? How can we get the good news out in our communities and sing the message from our rooftops?

Discussion

1 What do you think of when you hear the word 'mission'? Is that helpful or unhelpful? How might you try to explain it to someone outside of the Church?

2 Read John 20:21. What does it mean for the Church to be sent into the world in the same way Jesus was? What might that look like in practice?

3 What do you think is the connection between worship and mission and how does the former shape us for the latter?

2

Church on the move: Engaging with the world around us

I've already mentioned the church I attend in south London. It's an imposing Victorian building, situated opposite the hustle and bustle of Peckham Rye train station, right at the heart of a diverse and busy part of the capital city. When I first started attending in the late 1990s, the church building was in a fair state of disrepair, and the stone walls at the front were overgrown with bushes and weeds. This prevented much of the church from being visible to those walking down the street.

As the congregation began to grow (and there will be plenty more stories in this book about how that happened), those in leadership wanted the church building to appear more open and welcoming. A garden clear up project was begun and the large, unwieldy bushes at the front were cut back, revealing a Pandora's box of forgotten community – dirty needles, cans, nappies... and the odd shopping trolley. A shiny new noticeboard was erected, making clear to those who passed by that the church open and active, and they would be most welcome to attend. While good publicity won't exactly stem the decline we see in our Western culture today, the noticeboard certainly did its bit in announcing the church was alive and well in our little corner of Peckham, and through the doors, people did indeed begin to come.

Over time, as the church grew, Peckham itself started to change dramatically. Gentrification took root in this so-called up and coming part of town, and disused premises opposite the church became the site of cafés and upstart local breweries. What had been a thoroughfare to rush through on the way to somewhere else, turned into a place to hang out, and on a balmy summer's evening, hordes of young adults would spill out of the bar onto the street. It transpired that the newly exposed stone walls of the church were the perfect perching point for late night drinking. For a church desperate to engage with the younger generation, a generation largely absent in the established church, this new development brought things tantalising close. However, it turns out that Victorian stone walls aren't designed to bear the weight of boozing millennials, and over time they started to crumble and crack. The local council declared a health hazard and the site of a potential accident.

Keen not to fail in its social responsibility, and knowing it had to prevent the walls from causing anyone harm, the church leapt into action. Very few churches have pots of money sitting around for a costly repair job like this, so as a temporary measure, a hardboard barricade was put in place. Unfortunately, because people had been easily stepping over the walls into the area of land around the church, the barricade had to be high enough to prevent them having access at all. What had once said, 'Come on in' now said, 'Please keep out', which was perhaps not the best message to convey.

In its wonderful entrepreneurial way, the church addressed itself to the knotty problem of both maintaining the safety of the site and sending a 'You are welcome here' message. A talented local artist was commissioned to produce a bright and welcoming mural across the temporary hoarding, in a bid to express something of the church's vibrant presence in the local community. Over a period of days, eight metres of boards were lovingly and creatively painted with colours and images, and the final result was magnificent. As the sun set on Friday evening, everyone was pleased with this innovative solution to the conundrum, and I looked forward to friends of mine noticing this great artwork as they walked past.

By the following Sunday morning, the boards had been so entirely covered by the handiwork of local graffiti artists that there was not an inch of the original painting visible. Some of the graffiti was vibrant and attractive, while some of it displayed language decidedly inappropriate for the walls of a church. The decision was made to paint over the graffiti and to commission the local artist to recreate her beautiful artwork. But sure enough, the same thing happened once again, and the graffiti-covered temporary wall remained for a period of months – a manifestation of the local community well and truly putting its mark on the church.

In time, as money was raised, planning permission sought and new designs commissioned, the boards were taken down. Some were bought by church members keen to have a piece of unique Peckham artwork! Now, on top of the newly strengthened wall sits a metal railing with gentle wavy lines which seems to communicate nicely, 'Please don't sit on me' but also, 'You are welcome here'. The bushes continue to be trimmed and the shiny noticeboard is back.

Why all this talk about walls and fences?

Of course, walls have an important part to play in the biblical story. The walls of Jericho come tumbling down as a divine act in answer to repeated prayer. Nehemiah, commissioned to rebuild the walls of Jerusalem, weeps initially at the crumbling remains he finds. Paul uses 'wall' language in Ephesians to describe the human barriers we place between us, which are destroyed in God's creation of a new humanity in Christ. It would appear that as we go about the vital task of building a community of Christian people, some consideration of the metaphorical walls that we need either to build or to destroy is important.

I begin with the story above because I think it illustrates one of the tensions we wrestle with as missionary disciples. How do we relate to the community around us? What message do we want to send to those in our local area? How does the message of Jesus Christ relate to the twenty-first-century world in which we live?

The world we find ourselves in

We might think this is a particular challenge for the contemporary Church, but it's an age-old question. In the 1950s, an American theologian called Richard Niebuhr wrote what became a landmark book entitled *Christ and Culture*.[1] He sought to identify different possible ways in which the relationship between the Christian faith and contemporary culture could be understood. There are a number of flaws in his approach, but *Christ and Culture* nevertheless raises the significance of these questions for those of us involved in local churches and highlights some possible ways forward.

As Western culture becomes increasingly secular and pluralistic, building a Christian community gets even more challenging. Sociologist Callum Brown, in his aptly titled work *The Death of Christian Britain*, suggests that the chief characteristic of our contemporary context is the death of any sense of Christian culture and heritage.[2] Another sociologist, Steve Bruce, describes his understanding of the impact of that change (in particular, secularisation) upon the West:

> Christianity is now but a pale shadow of its former self. Rural churches are converted to houses; city churches become nightclubs and carpet warehouses; church commissions examine the entrails for signs of hope; and sympathetic commentators publish studies with titles such as *The Tide is Running Out* (Brierly 2000).[3]

The most recent statistics released from the Church of England present a similarly testing situation. National church attendance has fallen by 12% in the past decade, to less than half the levels of the 1960s. Around 40% of the church's clergy will retire in the next decade, and the average age of churchgoers is rising: 'An 81-year-old is 8 times more likely to be a church attendee than a 21-year-old'.[4] The all-female Swedish band, First Aid Kit, express well the mood of a secular society that has no need of God in their song 'Hard Believer', insisting that meaning does not come from any sense of the divine, and that the eternal and such things are just delusional.[5] With the death of a so-called Christian culture, the Church finds itself having to navigate an unfamiliar environment and being challenged as to how to respond.

Church and culture

I want to suggest that there are three main stances the Church can take towards this question of how it relates to its surrounding community. I'll explain these by referring to the three types of walls we encountered in the opening illustration.

1 'Like us please'

Some recent research undertaken on the general perception of the Church of England suggests that the vast majority of people are not aware of the presence of the Church in society. The best-case scenario seems to be that we are regarded with 'benign indifference'.[6] As witnesses of Jesus Christ, we know we have a great message to share, and we long for the Church to be seen as relevant to real people (and real-life situations) today. We want them to regard the Church as a joyful and hopeful place, as somewhere that might connect with their daily lives. As a result, we get caught up in the pursuit of relevance. Our view of culture may be that it's not particularly good or bad – but it can be plundered and used to communicate the gospel. So, a nice shiny noticeboard says, 'Notice us!' A funky mural says, 'We're not stuck in the dark ages'. How do we decide where to draw the line? Are there certain things we simply can't relinquish just to make the Church seem more accessible to people?

2 'Keep out'

I suspect there are not many people reading this book who think that the Church should have a 'Keep out' sign at the front. But can we unintentionally portray this message? It can sometimes be hard for newcomers to feel welcome in churches that have a strong sense of purpose and identity, especially if they are someone who's unfamiliar with particular ecclesial practices and behaviours.

A 'Keep out' stance acknowledges the tension we experience between the Church and the world, between the Spirit of God and the spirit of the age. As our culture seems to move further away from Christian values, we can slip into a fearful mindset – one that views the role of the Church as that of taking people away from the wickedness of the world into the safe haven of the Church. If we live with this perspective, culture has nothing to teach us; it is fallen and irredeemable. Do we then, as the Church, create our own new culture? There seems fairly reasonable biblical precedent for this idea. After all, wasn't Israel supposed to be a distinct community among the pagan nations? Doesn't Paul exhort us to 'shine like stars', being blameless and pure in a wicked and sinful generation (Philippians 2:15)? It could be argued that the greatest challenge in our postmodern culture is that of safeguarding the truth of the gospel. And the fact is that even if we might not articulate our 'stance' as being one of 'keep out', our behaviour and attitude can often communicate that very message.

One day, I invited a friend to church for a family celebration and was surprised that she looked uneasy. Not wanting her to feel awkward, I asked whether she was comfortable coming to church. 'Well,' she replied, 'I've never been before, and I didn't really think church was for people like me.' 'What do you mean?' I enquired, fascinated to hear just what kind of person she thought *was* welcome in church. She looked down and said, 'Well, I'm not a very good person, am I?' This conversation saddened me on several levels. First, I felt sad that my friend thought that her defining characteristic was that she wasn't a good person. I wanted her to know that she was made in the precious image of God and loved and treasured. And second, I felt even sadder that her assumption the Church would label her as 'bad' led her to presume she wasn't welcome. How have we managed to give the impression that Church is for those who have life sorted?

3 'Shape us'

Our third and final stance towards culture is exemplified in the church walls as a drinking spot and the graffiti artwork. In a desire to break down the barriers that have prevented people from feeling welcome in church, the message might be given, 'Come and put your mark on us'. This would indicate a welcome stance towards the changing culture as Spirit-inspired and a willingness to allow those changes to impact both the way Church is, and the message it seeks to deliver. The danger with this is that the Church is so keen to engage with the world around it, that it simply becomes a facilitator of the pervading worldview – more socially acceptable perhaps, but at the expense of remembering its distinctive identity and purpose.

While these three stances may seem to oversimplify what is actually a rather complex theological issue, they serve to demonstrate some of the tensions we find when engaging with the actual task of mission and discipleship, and point us towards a number of the deeper questions we have to address.

These may be explored on both a macro and a micro level. There is the broad matter of the Church's posture towards culture generally, and there are the day-to-day decisions we each face as Christians. This tension was brought home to me once in a conversation with friend who is a schoolteacher and one of the few Christian members of staff in their school. A fellow colleague had been talking about her interest in spirituality and suggested my friend read a book she had really enjoyed. The book was clearly written from a New Age perspective and would have had plenty of ideas in it that my friend would find problematic and that the Christian faith would indeed challenge. My friend was in a dilemma – should she take the book and read it? Or might that be an unwise thing to do as a Christian? And what about her friend? Would she offend her if she didn't take the book? These might not feel like huge questions about Church and culture, but they are representative of the situations we come across regularly. Our response is likely to be shaped by the position our own church might take. What would you do?

Before we suggest a way forward, let's look at some definitions.

Defining culture

The word 'culture' itself can be misleading. We used to refer to a 'cultured person' as someone who liked the finer things in life – classical music and fine wine rather than Xbox and fizzy drinks. But 'culture' actually extends to the whole of human life. The word comes from the Latin *cultus*, which means 'to care', and from the French *colere*, which means 'to till' (the ground). Martyn Percy comments that 'culture is, put simply, the study of what is overlaid, built or imposed on the natural environment.'[7] We are all cultural beings and cannot be understood apart from culture. This longer definition of culture by American theologian James D. Hunter is helpful. Culture is:

> a normative order by which we comprehend ourselves, others and the larger world and through which we order our experience. At the heart of culture is a system of norms and values … but these norms and values are better understood as commanding truths so deeply embedded in our consciousness and in the habits of our lives that to question them is to question reality itself.[8]

In theological terms, we might say that culture is what we make of God's natural creation. This means that some of our models, such as those suggested by Niebuhr's *Christ and Culture*, are problematic because they tend to presume culture is something external to the Church, rather than acknowledging we are all cultural beings and that, in different ways, our understanding of the Christian faith and the gospel are culturally influenced. There is no 'neutral' gospel or theology. An additional problem with such models is that they tend to assume that culture is either wholly good (so we should lower the walls and embrace it) or wholly bad (so we should build a higher fence). This vital question of how we understand and relate to culture is crucial if we are to be missionary disciples. Let's explore how the whole sweep of the gospel narrative encourages us to consider the matter.

In the beginning: Creation and the Fall

The first thing to note is that creation affirms the goodness of culture. Genesis teaches us that God makes everything. If culture is the means by which we understand ourselves and order our existence, then culture has always been a part of human life. When God sees the world he has made, he judges all things good (Genesis 1:31).

This has been one of the foundations of Christian art – an understanding that on the basis of Genesis 1 and John 1, the world is already laden with meaning and order. Trevor Hart writes:

The artistic imagination ventures forth, as it were, into a world believed to be already rich with actual and potential meaning, lays hold of materials whose natural qualities encourage some modes of handling and resist others, and, through a creative exchange with all this, renders the fruits of its interpretive labours into form for the benefit of those who, as yet, lack the eyes to see and ears to hear.[9]

Theologians have spoken of this idea in terms of common grace and general revelation – in short, that something of the nature and character of God is revealed simply in the way the world is. The Psalms remind us that God continues to look after and sustain creation:

You visit the earth and water it;
You greatly enrich it.
(Psalm 65:9)

An integral part of the creation narrative is that human beings are distinguished by being made in the image of God – *imago Dei*. At the heart of *imago Dei* is the idea that we are relational creations, designed to be in relationship with God, with one another and with creation. Those relationships have a particular way of representing and revealing God to the world. Jamie Smith suggests that the creation narrative presents us not with interesting facts about human anthropology, but rather gives us a sense of vocation, or, in his words, 'a commission that sends us into God's good but broken world with a calling'.[10] For Smith, this calling is three-fold.

First, we are called to 'image' God, as if 'image' were a verb rather than a noun. As God's image-bearers, Smith believes we are tasked with caring for creation, 'which includes the task of cultivating it, unfolding and unfurling its latent possibilities through human making – in short through culture.'[11] This idea challenges the sacred/secular divide which permeates much of our thinking in the Church. I remember being in a seminar where it was taught that the highest form of living was to be in full-time Christian ministry and if that wasn't what you were called to do, then your job was to earn money to fund Christian workers. This limited concept seems to fail to take note of the creation call to all people to image God. There is no place for saying the accountant is doing secular work, but the Christian minister is doing 'God's work'. We all have the capacity to image God in whatever work or non-work activity we do.

Second, Smith suggests that we are called to 'unfold creation's potential' and by this, he means that we are to be fruitful and multiply (Genesis 1:28). While creation is declared 'good' by God (Genesis 1:31), it is not yet complete; there is more to be grown, built and established. Part of the *imago Dei* is that we are to explore all the hidden possibilities in the world around us. Christians, therefore, are called to create public institutions, build business, start charities, be artists and writers. God, as Trinity, is revealed in both unity and diversity, and our creative acts in his likeness will also reveal that vibrancy and colour.

Third, Smith suggests that our calling as those made in the image of God is to 'occupy creation'.[12] By this, he means we are to recognise that all is not well in God's created world, and our task as Christians is to point to God's future coming. We will go on to explore this shortly.

The story of the Fall teaches us that culture has the potential to image God and hence lead us towards him in worship and wonder, but that it also has the potential to lead us away from God and image sin and destruction rather than goodness and hope. In Genesis 3, as humanity turns away from God, we see how all aspects of the world, including human life and culture, are impacted negatively. The task of stewarding creation, which was supposed to be entrusted to humanity, now becomes a source of trouble and pain (Genesis 3:17–19). Romans 1 points to the reality that the world around us (including culture) can give rise to idolatry and wickedness, diverting us from our intended purpose. The sixteenth-century Reformer Martin Luther is credited with the Latin phrase *homo incurvatus in se*, which translates as 'humanity curved in on itself', although the early church father Augustine also spoke about the 'inward curve' of sin. He believed that pride was the beginning of sin and that pride, at its heart, is turning away from God to ourselves. Ultimately, it is the misplacing of love, a choosing to love ourselves above God in a self-obsessed (rather than a healthy) way. It is this prioritising of self above others that leads to the destruction of our common life together.

This idea was illustrated perfectly in a story I read recently in a newspaper. A man on his daily commute in New York passed between two train carriages and, as he did so, his phone fell onto the train tracks. So concerned was he by this personal inconvenience, that he pushed the emergency stop button, bringing the entire train, packed full of commuters, to a stop. While I have sympathy for the loss of a phone and all the aggravation this causes, such behaviour seems indicative of an individualistic, turned-in-on-itself culture, which constantly feeds self-service and self-prioritisation to us through advertising and social media.

It is worth pointing out that Christians can quite easily emphasise the Fall too much in their cultural engagement. This creates a defensive posture towards the world around us and an assumption that 'everything' outside the Church is negative. I once spoke at a Christian conference and in the prayer meeting before the main session, someone interceded for the youth sessions taking place that day. I couldn't fault the heart of enthusiasm of the person as they prayed for 'the young people who are being brought up in a wicked and sinful generation', but I did question the theology. It is all too easy for the Church to adopt a retreat mindset when it finds itself in the minority. In fact, in times of persecution such a mindset might be helpful. However, missionally, it is problematic and leads to a posture of withdrawal and preservation. As we have seen, the creation narrative points to the dual capacity of culture – its ability to point towards God and its capacity to lead us away, because culture is ultimately what we make of God's world, and humanity itself is a mix of those two very things.

What is required, as we shall shortly see, is not an extreme stance of either total acceptance or total rejection, but the capacity for discernment.

Jesus and culture

Jesus has arguably featured in more famous works of art than any other historical figure over the last 1,500 years – from Da Vinci's *The Last Supper* and Michelangelo's vast fresco, *The Last Judgement* in the Sistine Chapel, to the twentieth-century masterpiece, *Christ of St John of the Cross* by Salvador Dali. However, Jesus is not only an object of interest in culture but is himself central to a Christian understanding of culture. As the one in whom 'all things in heaven and on earth were created, things visible and invisible, whether thrones or dominions or rulers or powers – all things have been created through him and for him' (Colossians 1:16), there is nothing that is beyond the reach of his influence. As the Alpha and Omega of creation (Revelation 1:8), Christ's death and resurrection are cosmic in scope, redeeming and forgiving all that is broken and sinful, while his resurrection from the dead is the first fruits of a new creation in which all culture will perfectly point to the love of God in him.

Trevor Hart explores the notion of Jesus as the incarnate Word of God, as expressed in John 1:14.[13] Hart points out that in Scripture, 'the Word', far from existing in some ethereal realm too sacred to be troubled with human concerns, is always spoken about in connection with the material world and the day-to-day activities of human beings. In countless Old Testament narratives, the Word of God is present in the world – not least in the miraculous events that guide Moses and provide food for the Israelites. The presence of the Word reaches its grand climax, of course, in the birth of Jesus, when 'the Word became flesh and lived among us' (John 1:14). In the act of incarnation, God chooses to make himself fully and definitively known in the person of Christ. In other words, God gets up close and personal. Christ's taking on human flesh is illustrative of our earlier point that culture is capable of both pointing us to God and away from God. In the incarnation, Jesus lives the perfect human life as a cultural being. He points to God in all he is and does, but he also steps into the fallen world to redeem and transform it, challenging human and cultural behaviours and attitudes which enslave and harm people rather than setting them free.

New creation

The resurrection is also significant to our engagement with culture. As the firstborn from the dead (1 Corinthians 15), Jesus is the pioneer of a new humanity, God's new community. By being 'in Christ', the Church is connected to this risen Christ, in that it is seen as the first fruits of the age that is to come. Just as Christ has been raised, we too will be raised. This is the great hope that missionary disciples have to share with the world today.

The Church inhabits what we might call 'in-between' times. Christians live in a world that has capacity for both goodness and evil, but we live with the future hope that one day Christ will return and set all things in their proper place. This is more than a 'pie in the sky when you die' kind of hope. It isn't a call to grin and bear it until it all works out. Jesus has inaugurated his new kingdom. We already live in the realm where Jesus is king and experience many of the blessings of that future age. And yet, we continue to live in hope that all things will be made new, when God's kingdom will be fully established on earth – 'as the water's cover the sea' (Habakkuk 2:14). To be a missionary disciple, then, is to be an in-between person.

One of my favourite viewing experiences was watching the TV series *Lost*. Its ground-breaking opening episode caught the nation's attention as it told the story of a horrific plane crash on a deserted island (or so we were led to believe!) in the Pacific Ocean. It was a striking piece of filming, and everyone was talking about it at work the next day. Losing all connection with the outside world, the survivors of the crash had to work out how to survive on the island which, it turned out, seemed to have some peculiar and potentially magical properties.

From the first episode, the drama used flashbacks as a way of filling you in on each character's story. I was hooked and devoured the first few seasons. However, as the show continued it began to get more complicated, operating on multiple timelines. In series 4, it introduced 'flashforwards' which showed certain characters a few years down the line, having been rescued from the island. Without wanting to give too much away (and apologies if I've now got you hooked on a six-season show you weren't aware existed), these flashforwards injected hope into the current reality. You knew this wasn't the end, there was a way out, a better future ahead – and you got a little glimpse of it every now and again.

As Christians, we experience flashforwards of God's coming kingdom. Seeing somebody healed, a miraculous answer to prayer, a person encountering Christ for the first time – these are all injections of hope into our present reality, pointing towards what is to come. We can be encouraged that God's future culture is breaking into our present culture!

In Ephesians 1:14, Paul uses the Hebrew term *arrabon* (a pledge paid as part of a payment owed, serving as a legal guarantee that the payment would one day be received in full) to describe the Holy Spirit. The Holy Spirit is the link between present and future realities. Our experience of the Spirit now, in both comforting and miraculous ways, is a pledge and a foretaste of all that is to come. This means, as Christians, we are in a relationship to culture that requires us to perceive what is fallen and belongs in the old age, and what is part of the new, knowing we have the mandate to create and build culture which speaks of the future hope we have in Christ.

Four principles for practice

What does this mean in practice for the Church, seeking to be a faithful witness in these in-between times, in the complexity of our current situation? Let's explore four principles for practice.

1 Discernment is our task

Hopefully, it is now clear that culture is neither wholly good nor wholly bad, and that the Church's relationship with culture is more complex than the taking of a single stand or position. We are living as future-present people in the in-between times, and working out how to navigate these times is a serious task. It requires, as I mentioned earlier, the capacity for discernment.

How do faithful disciples of Jesus Christ in the world today discern (both within and outside the Church) what works towards God's glory and what doesn't? Three words are important here.

Listen: The first stage in the task of discernment is that of listening to the world around us. If we're too concerned with self-preservation, we'll never become the prophetic future-present voice that we're imagining here. As a community, we need to be engaged in institutions, workplaces, networks and communities outside the hallowed walls of the church, simply listening and hearing what matters to people. Francis Schaeffer, one of the great apologists of the twentieth century, said:

> Christianity demands that we have enough compassion to learn the questions of our generation. The trouble with too many of us is that we want to be able to answer these questions instantly, as though we could take a funnel, put it in one ear and pour in the facts and then go out and regurgitate them and win all the discussions. It cannot be.[14]

If we don't listen to the questions people are asking, how will we even begin to answer them with the good news of Jesus?

It was with this in mind, that I strongly urged my teacher friend to read the book her colleague had given her. That way she could see what was important to her friend and begin to discern how to respond. Of course, we need to be sensible! I'm certainly not suggesting we recklessly and unthinkingly expose ourselves to everything culture might want to offer us. Our goal as disciples is always to draw closer to Jesus, so if reading or viewing something is not going to help us do that, we should leave it alone. I'm part of a film club with some local friends, and we watch a film every other month. There have been a couple of films I've declined seeing – one was too violent, the other was a horror-themed movie I just didn't feel comfortable about. But in the main, over eight years with this group, I've watched films that have made me think in different ways and have certainly opened up deeper conversations with my non-church friends. Listening, and prayerfully observing, is the first stage of discernment.

Affirm: As Christians, we can be known for being judgemental and quick to point out other's faults. It has often shocked me when I've been in conversation with people outside the Church that they automatically assume the Church is going to have a bad opinion of them. Jesus, who is judge of all, was never judgemental in his attitude towards people. In fact, when the man who was born blind came to see Jesus and the crowd assumed his disability was of his own making, Jesus was quick to point out that the man was not in any way to blame (John 9). It seems that Jesus reserved his harshest comments and critiques for the self-righteous religious folk who assumed they had life sorted. It's important, therefore, that we generously commend integrity, kindness and truth wherever we find it. Christians do not have a monopoly on goodness! During the pandemic, it was encouraging to see local churches responding to the practical needs of their communities, but there were plenty of other charities, local organisations and individuals offering care too. That's something to celebrate. Understanding that all cultures can be a source of goodness means that we can enjoy the insights and creativity arising from those different to our own, and sometimes we will find ourselves recognising goodness, beauty and wisdom in unlikely places. This is what we see Paul doing in Athens in Acts 17, as he listened to and appreciated the culture around him. Behaving in such a way demonstrates that the Church can be a generous and receptive community, keen to celebrate and work with others.

One church I know partners with a local (secular) charity which receives leftover food from local businesses so they can offer meals to homeless people or others in need in the local community. It's a partnership in which the church is happy to offer its building and equipment in order to collaborate with a non-church organisation and do something for the common good.

Critique: As Christians, we recognise that sin and injustice lurk in every culture and that it's important to speak out against wrongdoing on both a local and a national level. The criticism offered to church leaders when they dare to comment on politics or public matters – as if the Church should be resigned to the sphere of personal preference – can be frustrating. Nonetheless, the Church has an important role to play in challenging society when it fails to speak up for the marginalised.

Another church I know has partnered with a community organisation to champion the rights of those facing the unjust consequences of gentrification. It has sought to stand with, and indeed campaign against, the fat-cat global companies who seek to profit from the destruction of the livelihood of those in the local area.

This raises the question of how we know what to affirm and what to critique. Prayerful immersion in Scripture is the only way we can begin to discern how to respond to cultural challenges and changes as they come our way. (That's why, along with encouraging my teacher friend to read her friend's book, I urged her to keep reading her Bible.) By being soaked in the former we can discern how to respond to the latter. Small groups and home groups are so crucial in our churches because Sunday morning sermons alone are not enough to equip us in this task of discernment. Our engagement with Scripture must be immersive, consistent and prayerful.

2 The margins are our location

Our second principle relates to the shift in mindset required for the Church which is no longer a dominant presence within society. For the post-Christendom Church, moving from being the moral majority to holding a minority viewpoint can feel disorientating, particularly for those who have been Christians for a long time who fondly reminisce about when 'everyone' got married and baptised in church. It's particularly challenging when our models for mission and ministry are based upon an assumption that people will want to come to church. American missiologist Timothy Tennent puts it like this:

> The collapse of Christendom has left Western Christians in an uncomfortable position because most have no real preparation or precedent for how to live on the margins, counter to the culture. For the most part, we don't know

how to think about missions without ourselves being at the center ... Our long sojourn under the spell of Christendom has also meant that we find ourselves adhering to a rather domesticated version of the gospel.[15]

Tennent suggests that the Church needs to learn to live on the margins, away from the centre. From this place, the Church needs to 'learn how to occupy the cultural periphery with a prophetic authenticity'.[16]

In July 2023, a first-generation iPhone (from 2007) was put up for auction. Originally priced at around $599, it sold for $190,372.80 – three hundred times the original amount. Apple is undoubtedly one of the most successful global companies, being worth over three trillion dollars. Its founders, Steve Jobs and Steve Wozniak, subsequently became millionaires – or a billionaire, in the case of Jobs. They met in 1971, when Jobs was just a teenager. Initially, they bonded over their shared love of technology and pranks, messing around with tech together, pranking Jobs' school, ringing the Vatican and almost getting through to the Pope. Then they devised a 'blue box' which enabled them to make long-distance calls for free. Eventually, their experimentation and skill led to them developing the Apple 1 – the archetype of the modern computer. As is so often the case, real innovation happened away from the centre, in the obscure location of Jobs' parents' garage (though they moved into a custom-built office in 1978).

So much of the way we operate as a Church is about big programmes and strategies, and while these are important, sometimes the things with the greatest potential happen in unlikely and unusual settings. Jesus' conversation with the Samaritan women, which leads to 'many Samaritans' following Jesus, occurs in an obscure, out-of-the-way place, at an unlikely time and with an even more unlikely person (John 4:31–42). It seems God is often to be found on the margins, and on the margins, the miraculous may well occur.

I have a friend who is a personal trainer. He volunteers weekly in a hostel for men who have recently left prison, many of whom are battling addiction and other challenges in an effort to get their lives back on track. When my friend visits, he offers physical fitness sessions, but the context also gives him the opportunity to talk about spiritual wellbeing, to share the love of Jesus and to pray with many of the men too. The hostel is an out-of-the-way kind of place, overlooked by most, but God is at work there, bringing new life and restoration. Reflecting on this example of the Church living on the margins with prophetic authenticity, can you think of places in your local area where something wonderful might grow?

3 Translation is our language

We are familiar with the idea of 'translation' in the context of global mission. Hudson Taylor, a British Baptist missionary to China in the nineteenth century, is one of the foremost examples of enacting translation well. He dedicated himself to learning Mandarin before his initial voyage across the sea, and during his five decades of medical and evangelistic ministry, he learned many other regional languages, eventually translating the New Testament into the Ningbo dialect. For Hudson Taylor, this was a crucial part of his missionary approach, in contrast to others who believed that teaching English (or other Western languages) was the key to successful evangelistic mission.

In commenting on the role played by missionary translators in Africa, Lamin Sanneh, a renowned Gambian scholar, says this: 'Few things have done more to mitigate the dialectics of power and injustice than confidence in a God who looks kindly on identity of tongue and soil.'[17] Sanneh's central idea is that Christianity is a translation movement rather than a dogmatic system. In contrast to other religions, in which culture and dogma are more acutely linked, the Christian gospel has the power to be incarnated in different cultures throughout the world. This does not mean that the central message of forgiveness and new life in Christ changes – rather that how this might look and be lived out can vary from place to place, as local cultures are allowed to shape and impact its expression. Sanneh's argument is that it was through translating Scripture into local vernacular languages that the concepts of the gospel could be understood and take root within those cultures. This enabled the good news to sparkle and shine in fresh ways. He puts it like this: 'The gospel is capable of transcending the cultural inhibitions of the translator and taking root in fresh soil, a piece of transplanting that will challenge the presuppositions of the translator.'[18]

While the issue of language may not seem of great relevance as we face our missional task in the UK (although it may well be), this cross-cultural principle is nevertheless helpful as we recognise the increasing gap between Church culture and the mindset and ideologies of those outside the Church. We would do well to consider the work of translation as just as important as that of discernment. Guder writes:

> Mission is to be a continuing process of translation and witness, whereby the evangelist and the mission community will discover again and again that they will be confronted by the gospel as it is translated, heard and responded to, and will thus experience ongoing conversion while serving as witness.[19]

The narrative of the gospel is universal in nature, but the Church needs constantly to translate its message to the world around, seeking actively for connection points with the gospel story.

Starbucks is one of the most familiar coffee brands, with a symbol that's recognised far and wide. In many ways, it adopts an anti-contextual approach, in that you can be sure you'll be able to get the same coffee in the same cup wherever you are in the world. However, what's not so widely known is that in each location there are local variations which contextualise the coffee experience for the consumer. So, for example, in Tokyo, you could sample a Sakura Blossom Latte, a pink milky concoction inspired by the national cherry blossoms in springtime. In Mexico City, you could order a Ponche Navideño, a tea-based drink with hibiscus, cinnamon and sugar, served during the holiday period. In London, you might eschew coffee and get a good old English breakfast cuppa! The point is that contextual variations, which do not change the core of what a business is offering, do enable people to feel at home and build community. The gospel is, of course, far more significant than the flavour of your coffee, but this fairly trivial example demonstrates how, in our increasingly secular culture, we might communicate the gospel in ways that people can understand and relate to – with the possibility of the gospel taking root in places we might previously have ignored.

One of the exercises I get my students to do in their class on evangelism is to translate the concept of 'sin'. It's a word whose meaning we take for granted in the Church, yet it can be loaded with misconceptions and unhelpful associations for those outside. I am always impressed with the ideas the students come up with: one reflected on the concept of shame in certain cultures; another used the analogy of collecting cookies on your browser history which keep a record of every website you visit, almost as if they know your every private thought and action. It's a fun exercise that shows the importance of the task of translation in our everyday witness. However, translating the gospel is never an academic exercise worked out on a computer screen – it involves becoming part of those communities where the gospel is not yet incarnated. As Newbigin writes, 'True contextualization happens when there is a community which lives faithfully by the gospel and in that same costly identification with people in their real situations as we see in the earthly ministry of Jesus.'[20]

Where in your local community is the gospel is not being translated? Who are the people you could get to know and build relationships with? What might Church need to look like for the young people who live there? How could you translate the gospel to them?

4 Hope is our currency

Ted Lasso quickly became a hit when it graced our screens in 2020. It tells the story of an American football coach who gets a job coaching a premier league football club. Ted doesn't know the offside rule from a corner kick, but soon wins his way into the hearts of players and fans alike. With his relentless positivity and optimism, Ted is unusual as a TV protagonist. In the final episode of the first season, Richmond FC are in a perilous situation, fighting against the ever-successful Manchester City to avoid relegation. In a scene in the locker room before kick-off, Ted tells his players that people have warned him that the hope of winning can be a real killer. He pauses and then explains that, for him, the opposite is true – that it is the absence of hope that brings us down. Ted chooses to believe in hope.

At the end of 2021, the *Financial Times* shared the findings of a survey among the British public in which 55% of people revealed that they felt pessimistic rather than optimistic. The recent pandemic and the threat of a cost-of-living crisis were cited as significant factors. A few years on, with the cost-of-living crisis far worse than people expected, daily prices rising and many public sector workers regularly on strike, I imagine the percentage might have increased even more. In addition, over half of those interviewed felt pessimistic about the lack of unity in the UK and actually expected societal divisions to increase rather than decrease. It seems in Britain that Ted Lasso might be right, and a lack of hope is coming to get us.

'But in your hearts sanctify Christ as Lord. Always be ready to make your defence to anyone who demands from you an account of the hope that is in you,' writes Peter in 1 Peter 3:15. There is an assumption here that, as Christians, hope is our currency, that it will spill out of our lives in such a way that others feel compelled to ask, 'Why are you so hopeful? What is it that gives you hope?' Our missional task in today's complex culture is to be bringers of hope into the word around us – whether as a banker or a bus driver, a parent or a friend. Theologian Karl Barth expresses this powerfully: 'The community dares to hope in Jesus Christ and therefore it dares to hope for the world.'[21]

Collectively, the Church is called to be a vehicle of hope in a world that has lost its way. This doesn't mean that as missionary disciples we have to have all the answers (or that our churches should be thriving financially, or even be without leaky roofs) – rather that we should do our best to live authentically together. Graham Cray puts it like this:

Western, affluent, multi-choice cultures lack hope. The best they have to offer is more of the same, but the church in each locality is to be a sign of hope, because in its own life and ministry people around it should encounter a foretaste of the future Christ has secured, for that part of his creation within the new heavens and earth. Churches are to be imperfect pilot plants of God's future world.[22]

Andy is the rector of a church just outside Brentwood in Essex. When the 'Beast from the East' struck in 2018, heavy snow fell and temperatures plummeted resulting in many being stuck in their homes and the local schools having to close. The next day, Andy received a call saying that all the school lunches had been delivered as usual, but the schools couldn't cook them. What should they do? Andy immediately collected the meals and rallied some volunteers from the church who got the food into ovens. The church hall was opened up so they could welcome in the children who would normally get free school meals, ensuring they did not go hungry. The schools remained closed for the next three days, but the children were able to make their way through the blizzards to receive warm food and support.

This experience sparked the idea of finding a way of reaching out more permanently to the families in the local area who were really struggling to make ends meet and slipping into poverty. The church established a community supermarket, where local business donated leftover food and those who were struggling to provide for their families could come and choose what they wanted to take home. The following Boxing Day, Andy received a phone call from the local M&S store saying they had fifty-five turkeys, pots of gravy and hundreds of bags of vegetables left over. Could the church use them? The church community leapt into action and the next day welcomed queues of people to whom they distributed various needed foodstuffs. One man, whose children were coming to visit, couldn't believe that instead of basic chicken nuggets, he could give them a Christmas dinner. Another woman stood in the queue with tears in her eyes. 'I haven't been able to feed my family,' she cried. But she went home with a feast. In a small way, these luxury Christmas dinners were an illustration of the heavenly banquet to which all are invited.

As Christ's missionary disciples, we are to be bringers of hope, living our lives publicly and boldly, serving with compassion and drawing people into family from all walks of life. This is our prophetic task in this cultural moment.

Maybe it's not the hope that kills you but the hope that keeps you alive.

Discussion

1 What attitude towards culture does your church hold? Is it affirming or resisting?

2 What are the dangers of either seeking too much cultural relevance – or, on the other hand, failing to make connection with the world around us?

3 Where are the places in your local community that your church can bring the hope of the gospel?

3
Church as presence: Being a successful church

When I was at university I was involved with the Christian Union, and a friend and I decided to put on an event for people to find out about Christianity. We devised some attractive publicity material and posted this around the college, invited everyone we knew and pooled our limited student finances to buy some delicious cakes. We prayed and really believed that God would bring in spiritual seekers. The start time came and went and no one showed. We waited patiently for the next thirty minutes, when there was a knock on the door and a guy from the adjacent corridor poked his head in. Looking awkwardly into the empty room, he sheepishly admitted he had only come for the cake. So we gave him a slice of chocolate sponge and let him go on his way.

The following year, I was involved in organising another mission event at the university. This one was on a slightly larger scale, and we hired a venue for five nights which seated around seven hundred people. A guest speaker was organised and again creative publicity was put up around the university; we even had mugs and beer mats printed. Everyone was encouraged to invite their friends. And what happened? Night after night, the theatre was packed full of people listening to the talk and testimonies, and many responded to the invitation to follow Jesus. Ten years later, at a home group leaders' event in my house in a different city, I happened to serve a cup of coffee in a mug from this mission. The man who accepted it stunned me by saying, 'I became a Christian at that mission.' I hadn't even known we had been at the same university!

When we come to think about success and the Church, what does it mean? Is the second of these stories a success and the first a failure? And what is success anyway? Is it about how many people attend on Sundays? Is it about the output of a church or the number of people reached by its ministries? I have often found myself feeling awkward and uncomfortable when a church leader promotes themselves in terms of the numerical growth their church has experienced.

Should we heed the advice of David Bosch, a leading South African missiologist, who challenged the idea that evangelism is about numbers?

> Evangelism cannot be defined in terms of its results or effectiveness, as though evangelism has only occurred where there are 'converts'. Rather, evangelism should be perceived in terms of its nature, as mediating the good news of God's love in Christ that transforms life, proclaiming, by word and action, that Christ has set us free.[1]

We might prefer to speak about faithfulness to the creedal faith, prayer and devotion as markers of a successful church. There is the deeper question of whether success is a category we should even be using when talking about the Church. But before we move too quickly to dismantle the notion of success, it's important to give some consideration to the role of numbers when thinking about missional church.

Our current preoccupation with numbers stems largely from something called the Church Growth Movement, which originated in the 1960s in the United States and is associated with names such as Donald McGavran and Peter Wagner. The Church Growth Movement sought to use insights from social sciences and the world of business to create a disciple-making strategy that would grow the Church. It has been influential particularly in promoting what is called 'the homogenous unit principle' and the idea that people are more likely to come to faith among a group of like-minded people. We'll pick up that idea again in a later chapter.

However, should numerical growth be the goal of our church life? What would Jesus think of our preoccupation with numbers?

On the one hand, the desire to grow the Church numerically feels an appropriate response to Jesus' words at the Great Commission. The call to make disciples of Jesus is a ministry of multiplication. It echoes the parable he told about the great banquet: 'Then the master said, "Go out into the roads and lanes, and compel people to come in, so that my house may be filled"' (Luke 14:23).

It appears Jesus desires many to respond to this invitation, with the image offered being that of a house full to bursting with unlikely but welcome guests. Luke mentions that after Pentecost three thousand new believers were added. Surely aiming for numerical growth is not a bad thing? It is not that numbers matter per se, but numbers in this case represent people and we know people matter to God. More Christians hopefully means that there are more of us loving and serving our communities, more people introducing others to Christ. Numbers are always going to be something we quite rightly seek. A church which is serious about living out its missional identity will surely attend to the question of growth and numbers. Newbigin expresses this well:

> Anyone who knows Jesus Christ as Lord and Saviour must desire ardently that others should share that knowledge and must rejoice when the number of those who do so is multiplied. Where this desire and this rejoicing are absent, we must ask whether something is not wrong at the very center of the church's life.[2]

However, when it comes to the mathematics of the gospel, things are slightly more ambiguous, and the simple equation of 'more equals better' is not always applied. There are times when Jesus intentionally dismisses the large crowd and instead seeks out the one. He goes to the well at the height of the sun's rays to speak with the Samaritan woman (John 4:1–42). He wanders among the tombstones in the deserted region of the Gerasenes to set free a troubled man (Mark 5:1–20). Jesus tells a story of a farmer who has a hundred sheep. Counting them, he realises one is missing and leaves the ninety-nine behind to go in pursuit of the one who is lost. In a sense it is a ridiculous narrative: surely the shepherd should stay with the ninety-nine sheep he does have and cut his losses? Why venture out to find the one that is missing? From a business perspective, it makes little sense, but Jesus completes his parable with these words: 'there will be more joy in heaven over one sinner who repents than over ninety-nine righteous people who need no repentance' (Luke 15:7).

The ones always matter to God

God's heart is for the lost and the least, the burdened and the confused. Programmes and strategies which prioritise the masses and allow no space for the ones and the twos cannot reflect the missional heart of God.

At the peak of the first Covid-19 lockdown, the vulnerable in our communities were struggling to manage. With shopping hours restricted and online shopping slots in short supply, many were finding it hard to get what they needed. Among other charitable agencies, numerous churches quickly took action, doing what they could to ensure people did not go without the necessities.

My friend Ben co-ordinated a project for his church in Leicestershire, arranging food deliveries for over a hundred people in the community where he lives. One day, while making deliveries himself, Ben knocked on a door but received no answer. He tried again without success. Having other deliveries to make, he was aware of being against the clock, but something just didn't feel right. Ben rang the bell of the house next door but the person who answered said he had not seen his neighbour for a couple of days. Not knowing what else to do, Ben called the police and, on breaking into the flat, they found an elderly gentleman in an armchair, at near starvation and dehydration point. Thankfully, an ambulance soon arrived and the man was able to get the medical help he needed. The knock on his door saved his life. The ones always matter to God.

Furthermore, when it comes to numbers, we probably need to acknowledge that there are some contexts in which it is simply easier to grow things. Middle-class, socially mobile, urban contexts appear to be easier than estates or rural villages. Should the same measure be applied to all? The fact is it simply isn't a level playing field. The 'From Anecdote to Evidence Report' published in 2014 strikingly notes that churches with a paid youth worker are far more likely to grow their youthwork.[3] This is a great reminder of the importance of focused and intentional youthwork, something that has become a near national crisis in our churches. But what about those churches who would desperately love to employ a youthworker but can't conceivably raise the salary? As I said, it simply isn't a level playing field.

If numbers are not necessarily the most reliable or helpful way to reflect upon the effectiveness of the mission of the Church, what else might be a suitable measure? We all too easily inhabit a consumerist identity which leads us to believe that our worth is determined by what we have or what we achieve. Challenging that mindset will inevitably feel unsettling. The Apostle Paul helpfully shows us that not all that is of value is so easily commodified.

Success in Thessalonica

Acts 17 records the story of Paul's missionary trip to the city of Thessalonica, a major trading port and the capital of the Roman province of Macedonia in Northern Greece. Thessalonica was a place of cultural and religious pluralism, being both the centre of the imperial cult (the worship of emperors and their families as divine) and housing many other religious shrines and idols. Initially, Paul visits the synagogue and preaches the gospel. We learn that 'some' of the Jews are persuaded to follow his Messiah, but the larger group of new believers come from the 'The devout Greeks and not a few of the leading women' (Acts 17:4). So far so good.

It's beginning to look like a 'successful mission'. However, some decide to stir up trouble and, inciting mob violence, instigate a riot in the city and accuse Paul and Silas of defying the emperor (17:7). Paul and Silas are arrested and released on bail, but the new believers in Thessalonica believe it is too risky for Paul to stay and so persuade him to leave overnight. What first appeared to be a successful trip ends abruptly and unexpectedly.

We don't hear much more of Thessalonica in the book of Acts – only the occasional mention of a believer or two such as Aristarchus in Acts 27:2 – but in writing to this new Christian community, Paul clearly outlines what he considers to be the successes and failures of his time there.

The first letter to the Thessalonians is probably the earliest New Testament text, most likely written around AD 52, a year after Paul's sharp exit from the city. He is quick to set the record straight on what some might have seen as a failed missionary endeavour: 'You know, brothers and sisters, that our visit to you was not without results' (1 Thessalonians 2:1, NIVUK).

Had Paul heard that thousands had converted and flocked to the new church after he left? How did he define a 'good result'? This letter is one of the most beautiful presentations of what success might look like in Christian ministry.

A community of virtue

We always give thanks to God for all of you and mention you in our prayers, constantly remembering before our God and Father your work of faith and labour of love and steadfastness of hope in our Lord Jesus Christ.
(1 Thessalonians 1:2–3)

Paul's heart bursts with thankfulness as he writes back to the community he left so abruptly. Those few conversions among the Greek God fearers and 'prominent women' have clearly led to significant growth, and there is now a recognisable Christian church. However, what Paul is most thankful for is that the believers have become a community of Christian virtue. We are familiar with the triad of faith, hope and love, popularised at many weddings through the reading of 1 Corinthians 13, but this is the first time in the New Testament that these virtues are mentioned. For Paul, they are the defining characteristics of a successful church, the identity markers of what it is to be the Church of Christ. And it's not about size; it's about character.

Michael Gorman, a biblical scholar who has written about 1 Thessalonians, argues that what Paul commends in this fledgling church is that they not only believed the gospel Paul had preached to them but also embodied it in their life together. Gorman reminds us that the gospel is not purely a doctrine to be believed – it's a way of life to be entered into. Through turning away from idols to worship the true and living God, the Thessalonians became 'a living exegesis of the Gospel of God'.[4] The virtues of faith, love and hope, therefore, relate to the very nature of the gospel itself.

What is interesting to note is that faith, love and hope are not just inner characteristics but involve a practical outworking. Paul writes that 'faith' produces 'work', 'love' prompts 'labour', and 'hope' inspires 'endurance'. Christian holiness, therefore, is not passive but active. It is not about removal from the world but engagement in it. Gorman describes this holy engagement in the world in these terms:

a kind of participation in God that means participation in the world in a radically new way. Thus faith, love and hope have to do with the distinctive form of Christian participation in the world; they are not merely centripetal activities but centrifugal ones. In other words they have to do with witness, with mission.[5]

Furthermore, these characteristics of virtue are not individual but corporate. So much of our understanding of discipleship has been shaped by a modern/Enlightenment way of thinking which has elevated individualism and prioritised our own faith experience and personal discipleship. While this is important, and the call to 'come follow Christ' is certainly heard by each of us individually, there has often been too much emphasis on our own personal discipleship. We sing songs that are about me and my relationship with Jesus, with Church sometimes feeling like an optional extra to be embraced if one finds it helpful. But Paul reminds us in Thessalonians that discipleship itself is ecclesial; it is community-shaped not individualistic. Paul considers his mission trip to Thessalonica a success, not because of the individual conversions that took place, but because there now exists a community which embodies the gospel and demonstrates this through the faith, love and hope it shows. There is an echo here of the sentiment with which this book began and Newbigin's famous statement about the Church as the hermeneutic of the gospel. He went on further to say:

> I am, of course, not denying the importance of the many activities by which we seek to challenge public life with the gospel – evangelistic campaigns, distribution of Bibles and Christian literature, conferences, and even books such as this one. But I am saying that these are all secondary, and that they have power to accomplish their purpose only as they are rooted in and lead back to a believing community.[6]

Newbigin does not suggest that evangelistic activities are of no value, but that without the Christian community visibly demonstrating what the gospel means, many of our activities and words will fail to have any impact. Like the Apostle Paul some 2,000 years before, Newbigin believed that communities of faith, love and hope have the power to change the world.

It is worth drawing attention to the fact that the virtues Paul talks about have both indicative (what the Church is) and imperative (what the Church should do) elements. As we've seen, Paul begins his letter by stating that he has heard the Thessalonian Christians are a community of faith, love and hope. This is a statement of their identity; of who they are. Paul also presents them with the challenge of continuing to grow more wholly into this identity. He ends his letter by saying, 'put on the breastplate of faith and love, and for a helmet the hope of salvation' (1 Thessalonians 5:8). The Thessalonians are already loving, faithful and hopeful, but they are to endeavour to become those things more fully every day.

The way Paul communicates Christian character here is typical of his teaching about ethical living in the New Testament, and it revolutionised my own discipleship during my early twenties when I was a Christian student worker in London. One autumn, I had to prepare a series of talks on Ephesians for a weekend away with the Christian Union. These particular students were passionate and committed followers of Jesus; they seemed to be deeply charismatic and to love extended times of worship and prayer, often seeking out experiences of the Spirit and words of knowledge for one another. But there was something slightly other-worldly about them, and I wondered how to bring them down to earth a little, to encourage their missional heart for their neighbour. In fact, I was beginning to realise that the desire for extended times of worship and prophecy was not shared by all, and divisions were beginning to form within the group. As I studied the book of Ephesians, I saw that the way Paul talked about living in the world spoke directly into their situation.

In writing to the church in Ephesus, Paul presents the Christian gospel of salvation as a precious gift given by God in Christ, and as a wonderful miracle which God achieves in Christ where Jew and Gentile are united in a new family. The first three chapters of Ephesians explore in great depth the nature of this gift, while the following three concentrate on its practical outworking.

It became clear to me that Paul doesn't write, 'God has done this for you, now you should do this for him', as if holiness were gained through some sort of reciprocal action. Holiness, rather, is living out of the reality that is already ours in Christ.

> I, therefore, the prisoner in the Lord, beg you to lead a life worthy of the calling to which you have been called, with all humility and gentleness, with patience, bearing with one

another in love, making every effort to maintain the unity of the Spirit in the bond of peace.
(Ephesians 4:1–3)

Spiritual realities of salvation, grace and redemption find true expression in the everyday realities of relationships and community. Christian discipleship isn't about striving for perfection and failing; nor is it about chasing spiritual experiences which remove us from the world. It's about living out the fullness of our identity in Christ in the communities he has placed us in. Loving our neighbour is not a duty but an outworking of the calling of the children of God.

This way of viewing Christian virtue is the way Paul views community in 1 Thessalonians. He uses three phrases which demonstrate the core virtues of the Christian community (faith, love and hope) and then shows how each of these is to be lived out more fully and authentically. Let's take them each in turn.

Work of faith

The word 'faith' is often used interchangeably with the word 'belief', but in Paul's world, the Greek noun *pistis* carries the connotation of faithfulness and would more accurately be translated as 'faithful allegiance' or 'trusting loyalty'. Paul recalls how the Thessalonians had 'turned to God from idols, to serve a living and true God' (1 Thessalonians 1:9). This turnaround would not have been without opposition or challenge. Paul knew that faith in Jesus was costly and contested and required dedication and loyalty. This is precisely what he sees in the Thessalonians, that 'in spite of persecution you received the word with joy' (1:6). Such verses are challenging to us Christians in the comfortable West, who might face ridicule or mocking for our faith but little that can be classed as 'persecution'.

In my work, I've been privileged to work alongside those training for ministry who have come from parts of the world where they have been imprisoned for their faith. It is sobering and humbling to hear their stories. May we, like those brave Christians, not lose our nerve, but rather show the kind of personal devotion and corporate dedication to faith that characterised the early church in Thessalonica.

Labour prompted by love

Paul, of all people, knew that being a disciple of Christ was hard work. Looking back on his abrupt exit from Thessalonica, he was only too aware of the challenges and difficulties to be faced. Yet his heart is warmed as he hears of a church that is characterised by love. Christian love like this is not an emotional response, an ephemeral feeling, but something born in labour and hard work, service and commitment. It's the love that arranges a birthday party for the person in the community who has no one to celebrate with, the love that sits patiently with a friend at a hospital appointment as they wait for news, the love that asks, 'How are you?' and stops long enough to hear the answer. It's the love that shows the gospel being lived out in practice.

Henri Nouwen was a Dutch Catholic priest, a professor and a psychologist who spent his latter years serving in L'Arche Daybreak community in Canada among those who had intellectual disabilities. A prolific author, one of his most profound and personal works is *Life of the Beloved*, which emerged from a close friendship he had with a secular Jew called Fred. Fred asked Nouwen to write a book about spirituality that he and other secular professionals could understand. Here's an extract:

> Fred, all I want to say is 'you are the beloved' and all I hope is that you can hear these words spoken to you with all the tenderness and force that love can hold. My only desire is to make these words reverberate in every corner of your being – 'you are beloved'.[7]

Nouwen expresses so beautifully what defined the Thessalonian church, and what must be the beginning and end of every expression of Christian mission: the love of God.

Steadfastness of hope

It is interesting that Paul ends his triad with hope, whereas later versions of this triumvirate have love in the final position. The fact is that Paul sees steadfastness in hope as ultimately characterising a successful Christian community: hope in the face of opposition and adversity, hope which radiates outwards and becomes known by others, hope in a Jesus who will return.

Sue was a friend of mine from church who was diagnosed with cancer in her early seventies. She was one of those people who had a remarkable testimony of how God had intervened in her life as an adult and set her free, and she loved telling others about him.

A couple of days before she died, my friend Emma and I had the privilege of visiting Sue in the local hospice. She looked so small in her huge hospital bed, but her face beamed with joy as we arrived. She proceeded to tell us about all the people she'd been praying for; in fact, staff had made a point of gathering in Sue's room at the end of the day because it seemed such a hopeful place. She made me laugh with her story of the Anglican chaplain who had come and offered to pray for her and been somewhat taken aback when Sue said afterwards, 'Right, now let me pray for you,' reached out her frail arms and laid hands on him to be filled with the joy of the Spirit. She told me, 'I simply prayed that the Lord would bless his socks off!' He commented that no one had ever prayed for him quite like that before! Sue's hope in Jesus was infectious, and while she was very sad to leave her family behind, she could not wait to see Jesus face-to-face. Her steadfast hope humbled and encouraged me.

And so, if the Apostle Paul is right, the mark of a successful church is the embodiment of the gospel – a community living in love, faith and hope in a world awash with anxiety and tragedy, with the hope of the world being transformed. Or, to express this rather more personally, what matters more than our strategy to get people into church, modernise our worship or update our buildings – as important as those things are – is faith, love and hope.

Four principles for practice

What might that mean for us? Here are four principles for practice.

1 Success is about Mondays not just Sundays

In my final year at secondary school in Handsworth in Birmingham, my friend Esther and I took on the leadership of the Christian Union. It was an all-girls school, and a handful of us used to meet on a Wednesday lunchtime for prayer and Bible study together. Over time, girls started to invite their friends, and as we began to discern a hunger to experience God, we introduced worship and times of ministry, asking God to fill us with the gifts of the Spirit. Week by week, our little gathering grew until we were positively bursting out of the geography classroom! So keen were these new believers to pray and worship that it was quite a struggle to finish the meeting at 1:30 p.m. and let everyone get to their afternoon tutor groups in time. We felt as if we were experiencing a mini-revival and were so encouraged by what God was doing.

One day, Esther and I were summoned to see the headmistress. She had received complaints about the loud singing coming from the geography room and reports that girls were often returning to their classrooms in tears after our Christian Union gatherings. Esther and I respectfully explained to her that all we were doing was praying together and worshipping, and that tears of joy were perfectly natural when you receive the Holy Spirit. She listened to our response, took a sharp breath and then shouted in exasperation, 'But Christianity is for Sundays!' Thankfully, after some negotiation, we were allowed to continue our gatherings. But we had to tone down the exuberant worship and make sure we finished early so the girls had time to wash their faces before they returned to class.

It has often been the case that our mission activity as a Church has been focused on Sundays, the common pattern being that we meet people in other contexts and invite them to church. Thankfully, since the Mission-Shaped Church report in 2004, there has been much more emphasis on expressions of church that are not necessarily Sunday-focused, and do not have the ultimate goal of feeding into Sundays. The Church that seeks to embody the gospel needs to live out its life of faith, love and hope every day of the week and in every location where people of the Church gather.

The Anglican Communion service expresses this kind of idea in its post-eucharistic prayer, 'Send us out in the power of your Spirit to live and work to your praise and glory.'[8] As a child, hearing that prayer was one of my favourite moments of my weekly church experience (I think because it signified the end of the service and the tantalising promise of a custard cream!), and the prayer remains dear to me to this day. It reminds us that, like those first disciples on Pentecost day, we are gathered in order to be sent out; that church is more than our collective worship; that each Sunday we receive encouragement to be passionate about living out our discipleship in our places of work, education, leisure and at home.

This raises the question of how effective our churches are at equipping people to live out their missional calling, particularly in those contexts where it might be challenging to speak about the Christian faith. One of the reasons sociologists give for the decline in church attendance during the twentieth and twenty-first centuries is what is called a 'plausibility gap' between what happens on a Sunday and what goes on during the rest of the working week. In an increasingly secularised society, church attendees may find their faith being unable to encompass the questions and issues raised in their places of work. Those of us with responsibility for teaching and preaching must think about how we address this. For a while, my church had a regular item as part of the Sunday service called 'This time tomorrow', when a member of the congregation would be interviewed about what they would be doing on Monday morning. It was a helpful way of making a connection between our gathered worship and our sent-out worship.

2 Success is about holistic witness

In thinking about mission, we can become preoccupied with productivity and effectiveness. We might find ourselves assuming (or feeling) that it is the job of the Church to sort and solve everything. However, Sam Wells, in his book *Incarnational Mission:*

Being with the world, challenges our fixation with problem-solving.[9] Mission can so easily become about the Church 'doing', that we forget about 'being'. Instead, Wells suggests, we might look at the goal of mission as that of 'being with' people. The book's central idea of the gospel as Immanuel – God being with us – resonates with me. It seems to make sense of those situations where we're faced with problems that seem unfixable. If our modus operandi is that we always have to do something or always have to come up with a solution, have we failed when we find we can do neither?

Let's return to Paul: 'But we have this treasure in clay jars, so that it may be made clear that this extraordinary power belongs to God and does not come from us' (2 Corinthians 4:7).

Paul is writing about the gospel of light which reveals the glory of God. He reminds us here that the vehicle God has chosen to 'house' this dazzling treasure is not a shiny gold vase encrusted with sparkly jewels, but an ordinary clay jar, an image of fragility. As Paul frequently reminds us, it is through our weakness that the power of the gospel is made known. There is a sense of disproportion between the thing that is offered and the one offering it. Our weakness is no hindrance to the demonstration of God's power and grace.

The truth of this was impressed most firmly upon me during my first experience of prison ministry. I turned up early to meet the chaplain as agreed, and he showed me the locker where I had to leave my keys, wallet, phone and, in fact, all my personal belongings. On his advice I had dressed plainly in simple (rather boring!) clothes. I felt strangely vulnerable and exposed. The prison was still on a strict lockdown regime and the men were in their cells for 23.5 hours of the day. Our visits consisted of standing at the doors and asking if they wanted a chat or someone to pray with.

On the first couple of visits, I felt completely out of my depth. I normally consider myself quite good at small talk and can start a conversation easily with people at the bus stop or in the queue at the supermarket, but here, through a closed door in an unusual environment, I was struggling to make connections. All my usual starting points seemed irrelevant and my privileged experience felt far removed from these men's current reality. And so, I started to pray, 'God help me. I feel out of my depth. Show me what to say.' Gradually I found the words. The treasure began to break out of the jar of clay, and as I prayed through the door of a cell with, on a number of occasions, grown men weeping on the other side, I experienced some of the holiest and most precious encounters of my life. At that moment, all the things I might usually rely on to give me confidence – my education, my job, even my colourful clothing – counted for nothing. All I had was the powerful presence of God, and, as it turned out, that was all I needed.

What Paul commends the Thessalonians for is not their productivity or output but their presence. Despite the challenge and opposition that they faced, their community embodied love, faith and hope – the very things which the world so desperately needs.

In his book, *Finding the Church*, Daniel Hardy suggests the following four characteristics as a good test for the health of a congregation:[10]

- *Intensification:* First, he asks whether the church is being formed by the gospel. Is it growing and are people maturing in their faith in Christ? If people aren't growing, then the church might not be as healthy as it imagines.
- *Range:* Second, he asks the church to consider how attentive they are to important global issues. Is there an awareness of life beyond the walls of the church? Is the church able to 'read the times' and know what issues are important to people, or is it stuck in its own cocoon, hiding away from global realities?
- *Affinity:* Third, he asks, how close is the church is to those in the vicinity? Do people have relationships with those nearby? Are they concerned with the hearts and minds of others?
- *Mediation:* The last characteristic Hardy suggests is about the way in which all these elements of intensification, range and affinity are drawn together, 'placing the intensity of the gospel in the closest affinity to those lives and societies to which it is addressed.'[11] Mediation is the way in which the gospel message is brought into connection with the specific context the church is in.

It is interesting that, for Hardy, the Church's proximity to others is part of its health. We can tend to assume that the Church is stronger when it retreats from the influence of the surrounding culture, but here the test of its health is the extent to which it listens, understands and responds to the needs of those round about. This level of affinity is only gained through proximate presence, being up close and not keeping our distance.

And so, it is good for us to ask ourselves, how present are we in our communities? Do we gather where people are? Do we have a presence in public spaces?

Yet we might also ask, are presence and proximity all that are required? The common phrase, 'Preach the gospel and if necessary use words,' is often attributed to St Francis of Assisi, though it is almost certain St Francis did not say this. Nevertheless, it is a provocative statement that helps us think about the way the gospel is communicated to people. It challenges the perception that evangelism is all about words and properly identifies lifestyle, character and presence as powerful parts of Christian witness. However, it also potentially creates a false dichotomy between words and actions, supposing that the former are somehow secondary and only to be used when necessary. The reality is that the Church's witness has always been about both word and action. Paul writes to the Thessalonians about their 'labour of love' (1 Thessalonians 1:3). The character of love leads to action. Steve Aisthorpe puts this beautifully: 'Love is a noun that longs to be a verb.'[12] The love of Christ is demonstrated in words and actions. Success is about holistic witness.

The story is told of the church father Jerome, who undertook the task of translating the Gospels into Latin in the fourth century – no doubt a complex and arduous task. When persecution struck and the Christians in Rome had to flee, it is said that Jerome dropped the manuscript he was working on and was heard to utter, 'Today we must translate the words of Scripture into deeds, and instead of speaking saintly words, we must act them'.[13]

This synthesis of word and action has always been at the heart of what it is to witness to Christ. Words without actions are meaningless (like a clanging gong, as Paul would go on to say in 1 Corinthians 13), but actions without words cannot bring the lifesaving message of the gospel. 'How can they hear if they have not been told?' Paul asks in Romans 10. It's not a case of pitting words against actions. We are called to both. And in the synthesis of the two, the love of Christ is made known.

Not far from my house is the national training college for the Salvation Army. It's an impressive building (and a well-known landmark in Denmark Hill), with statues outside of William and Catherine Booth, two individuals who embody this commitment to word and action going hand in hand. One of the early mottos associated with the Salvation Army, which demonstrates the correlation between acts of service and witness, was 'Soup, Soap and Salvation' (a motto I have also found helpful in the raising of three teenage sons!) However, it is important we don't take for granted that one affects the another. Serving someone's physical needs does not 'win us the right' to speak to them about Jesus – doing so could be manipulative and harmful. We love, not to put others in our debt but, as John, known as the Apostle of Love, reminds us, 'because he first loved us' (1 John 4:19). The motivation to show love to others comes from our own experience of God's grace and not from the hope of gaining from our action. In an increasingly secular society, I predict it will be important for the Church to be clear about this. On occasion, I've felt uncomfortable when people have been invited to one thing and it has turned out to be something different. Or when people have thought they were simply receiving a meal and then found themselves being preached at. While we need to 'take every opportunity' to share Christ, it is important we do so with integrity, being honest with people about what they can expect.

A friend of mine is involved in a café for refugees in the south of England. Volunteers from the church come to cook and serve alongside those who are learning vital catering skills, in the hope that they may be able to find employment. No direct evangelism takes place as the goal of the kitchen is to meet a physical need – the training and equipping for work. However, the natural and loving way in which the church volunteers go about offering their assistance has, on many occasions, prompted people to ask them about their faith. Some of the refugees, initially prompted through this unspoken witness of the church in action, have attended church on Sundays or even responded to Christ and been baptised.

Jürgen Moltmann, a German theologian, writes about the dichotomy between words and actions:

> In many Christian churches ... polarizations have come into being between those who see the essence of the church in evangelization and the salvation of souls and those who see it in social action for the salvation and liberation of real life. But in Christian terms evangelization and humanization are not alternatives ... Nor are the 'vertical dimension' of faith and the 'horizontal dimension' of love for one's neighbor and political change.[14]

Like Paul, Moltmann believes that gospel witness involves both speaking and doing, presence and action. Embodying the gospel means that it impacts and shapes every aspect of our life as the Church. Embodying the gospel means that polarisations between evangelism and social action, pastoral care versus mission, or worship versus outreach do not make sense. The Church that embodies the gospel must do so with both words and actions, being present in all the forgotten corners of our world.

3 Success is about the common good not just conversion growth

You might be forgiven for thinking I have an obsession with walls! However, there is one more wall story I want to share. In the summer of 2011, riots broke out in different parts of London, after the police shooting of Mark Duggan, a twenty-nine-year-old Black British man living in Tottenham, north London, who was wrongly suspected of carrying a gun. I clearly remember the moment the riots started in Peckham. My youngest son was just days old and my mother-in-law had come to visit to help out. She had kindly offered to take the older two (five and seven years old) to see *Cars 2* in the cinema in Peckham and, not knowing the area very well, I had drawn her a map with the route to the cinema in the middle of Peckham. I told my eldest to show his Nana the way we walk to church (which was close by).

Two and a half hours later, I was expecting them home and listening out for their usual shouts as they came down the street. Instead, I became aware of a loud whirring noise that seemed to be getting louder and louder, and when I looked out the window, I saw a police helicopter circling not far away. I opened the front door to check anxiously if there was any sign of the boys and Nana, and was assailed by police cars, ambulances and fire engines rushing past with blue lights flashing and sirens blaring. All the while the helicopter circled, getting closer and closer, and I confess I started to panic.

Then suddenly three figures appeared in the distance, making their way down the street towards the house. The boys rushed towards me, breathless in their enthusiasm to tell me all about Lightning McQueen's latest adventure and blissfully unaware of their surroundings. I hurried them inside and switched on the TV, sensing something significant was unfolding. Local news showed footage of riots in various parts of London, shops being looted, buildings set on fire. I later discovered that a group of people with Molotov cocktails were making their way up Rye Lane towards the cinema, and my boys and their Nana had missed being caught up in the mayhem by a matter of minutes.

It was a stressful and sorrowful night as we watched events on our news screens and heard stories of local shops and businesses being ransacked and burned. People were seen running down the road carrying boxes of brand-new trainers and bags of Basmati rice. Tensions and emotions ran high, and anger raged on both sides.

But what happened in Peckham over the next few days was unexpected. As people ventured onto Rye Lane where previously there had been fires, and where shattered glass and broken shopping trolleys still lay strewn about the place, they started to gather around the Poundland store. Of all the properties of Rye Lane that had had their windows smashed (and temporarily boarded up),

Poundland was one of the largest. A group of local people were handing out sticky notes and pens, asking local residents to write how they felt about recent events. The response was astounding as a handful of messages grew into over 4,000 individual sticky notes, including those of local dignitaries and politicians. Some of the messages were of a political nature and condemned what had taken place, but the vast majority were declarations of love for Peckham. Kids and adults alike were scrawling affirming messages on sticky notes, such as 'Proud of Peckham', 'This is my home' and 'Peckham sparkles, come catch the shine'. Many of the messages declared God's love for Peckham or expressed a desire for God to bless the area. By the end of the week, seven boards were covered with beautiful affirmations of Peckham and, in time, the messages were digitised. They remain a permanent monument to a message of beauty and hope in the midst of tragedy and fear.

In their book, *Stay in the City*, Gornick and Wong speak of the importance of Christians who live in urban spaces being 'for' the common good of the city.[15] It is not enough to focus on the church's own life, building and community. A church that wants to embody the love, faith and hope of the gospel needs to seek the flourishing of the world around it. Gornick and Wong express it like this:

Cities are part of God's creation, intended for the flourishing of people and all realms of life. The thriving of cities depends upon the involvement of all. We can share in the work of cities by learning about them, finding ways to participate in their life, and assessing what we can do for the peace of God's world in light of our Christian convictions. As we stay in the city we can learn to love it, care about its future, and join with others in creating and praying for a more flourishing urban world for all.[16]

Of course, this is not to say that Christians shouldn't also seek the flourishing of rural places, but there is something particular about the way that cities function. As urban Christians, we may find it possible to retreat and live an isolated life, caught up in the interests of our church, trying to build, in effect, our own Christian city within the city, with the goal being purely about numerical growth. However, while numerical growth is important, as we have seen, it cannot be the sum total of our missional aim. Jesus reminded his disciples that they were the 'salt of the earth' (Matthew 5:13), having a preservative function in the life of the world. We are called to be beacons of God's hope, seeking signs of his goodness and grace and enabling others to know and live in peace.

Through Jeremiah, God reminds his people, carried off into exile, that he has not forgotten them and that they are not to retreat, but are to seek the good things God is doing: 'seek the welfare of the city where I have sent you into exile, and pray to the LORD on its behalf, for in its welfare you will find your welfare' (Jeremiah 29:7).

Gornick and Wong suggest that, instead of focusing on our own personal discipleship and church growth in order to transform the city around us, we should seek the common good of the city around us, and that might actually create the environment in which we can effectively grow a church and live as faithful disciples of Christ. This is part of our response to the *missio Dei* – that we seek and discern the places in our cities, towns, villages or rural communities where God is at work in order to join in with what God is already doing to bring about a kingdom of righteousness.

And so again, we might ask ourselves where there are opportunities to seek the welfare of our cities or rural locations. What is going on locally that we might get involved with, simply to be a blessing to those around us? Perhaps you might join a local conservation society, a welfare agency or a charity that is campaigning for issues that matter to local people. Perhaps you could muck in on a local litter pick. If we have the courage to look beyond the goal of numerical growth and see ourselves as those who are called to embody and live out the gospel of Jesus, we will find such things become part of our missional calling. And who knows, they might even grow the Church too!

4 Success is about faithfulness

John Wesley is one of my spiritual heroes. Born in Epworth in the Midlands in the early eighteenth century, his father was an ordained clergyman in the Church of England and his mum, Susannah, a formidable source of spiritual nurture and encouragement, especially in his early years. The Church of Wesley's day was not entirely unlike our own, being in crisis, with fewer people attending, the rise of science and rationalism presenting new challenges to the idea of faith, and an increasing number of church buildings and livings to maintain. However, it was also a season of new opportunities and innovation and emphasis on personal choice. It was a time of contrasts, as Dickens described:

> the best of times, the worst of times, it was the age of wisdom, it was the age of foolishness, it was the epoch of belief, it was the epoch of incredulity, it was the season of light, it was the season of darkness, it was the spring of hope, it was the winter of despair.[17]

At this moment of crisis in the Church, Wesley and others like him preached a courageous message of personal repentance and faith in Christ. This message was so refreshing and new, accompanied as it was by manifestations of the Spirit and the call to respond personally, that thousands would gather in churches and public buildings (or fields and open spaces when there was no room inside). It was a watershed moment in the Church in Britain, leading to a nationwide movement of revival and transformation.

As the figurehead of the revival, Wesley attracted droves of people to hear him wherever he turned up to preach, often having ridden hundreds of miles on horseback to get there. One gathering was particularly significant for Wesley personally – at Epworth in Lincolnshire. Wesley had been born in the vicarage there and was only a young boy when a fire had broken out. All the children – there were lots of them, Susannah gave birth to fifteen babies in total! – escaped from the burning house, except for John. Known affectionately to his parents and siblings as 'Jacky', he appeared at an upstairs window, crying for help. His parents, fearing it was too late, fell to their knees and prayed for their precious boy. Some men from the village gathered and, standing on one another's shoulders, reached up to the window just in time and managed to rescue Jacky before the roof caved in and the entire rectory was engulfed in flames. Wesley's tomb contained the epitaph, 'a brand plucked from the burning', and he always had a sense of being saved for a particular purpose.

It must have been moving to return to the scene of his childhood and to preach in the very church his father had done some thirty years previously. As I mentioned earlier, it would have been typical of many established congregations of its time – apathetic and dispirited and, despite the popularity of his mother's somewhat unorthodox kitchen Bible studies, experiencing little apparent fruitfulness and growth. In 1742, John's reputation as an 'enthusiast' had preceded him, and he found himself *persona non grata*. Despite offering to preach, he was not welcome and so decided instead to minister outside the church on his father's tombstone, after the evening service had finished.

Wesley stayed in Epworth for several days, sharing from his father's graveside the good news of Jesus Christ and the forgiveness of sins available to all. Crowds began to gather from far and wide, eager to hear and respond to his message of new life in Christ. On his final night of preaching, on 13 June 1742, Wesley recorded this in his diary:

> At six I preached for the last time in Epworth churchyard (being to leave the town the next morning), to a vast multitude gathered together from all parts, on the beginning of our Lord's sermon on the Mount. I continued among them for near three hours; and yet we scarce knew how to part. O let none think his labour of love is lost because the fruit does not immediately appear! Near forty years did my father labour here; but he saw little fruit of all his labour.[18]

What Wesley knew in that moment was that God required his faithfulness, just as God had required the faithfulness of his mother and father some forty years earlier. Fruitfulness was down to God, not technique or charisma. We must do all we can to think creatively and strategically about mission and have the courage to change and adapt our practice as need be – but sometimes there is simply no reason why some things are more 'successful' than others. Leading Latin American theologian Samuel Escobar writes:

> If Christian mission is first and foremost God's mission, Christians must always conduct mission in an attitude of humility and dependence on God. When the human dimensions of the missionary task overtake and determine the way in which mission is conducted, mission becomes human activity without redemptive power.[19]

If we aim for numbers or focus on our own activity in mission we run the risk of losing sight of the one whose mission it ultimately is. Success is not down to us. God does not judge us by numerical growth or the number of people we have led to Christ. What he requires first and foremost is our dependence upon him, which is borne of prayer and reliance upon the Spirit.

Discussion

1 Contemplating this this chapter as a whole, do you think numbers are something we should aim for in mission?
2 Reflect on faith, love and hope as the three core Christian virtues. What would it look like for the Church to embody those characteristics more?
3 In what way could your church contribute towards the common good in your local area?

4

Church as community: Being the body of Christ

Claire and Matt were committed members of their local church in a large city. Matt was involved in Sunday school, teaching and discipling the children, while Claire was on the outreach team. She regularly visited people in need in the local area to pray with them and often shared her faith with others. The couple were committed and faithful members of the congregation, giving both their time and money generously, while their two young children loved the children's activities and all-age services.

Then a job opportunity came up for Matt on the south coast and they moved down during the summer. They tried their local church, but it felt really small compared to the vibrant one they'd been part of in the city. There weren't so many activities and the kids got bored. There was another church further out of their village, but they found the theology there uncomfortably narrow. They travelled to the next town where there was a larger church: the kids loved the activities, but the worship felt chaotic and too informal, and Claire and Matt didn't really get to know anyone. They started attending less and less, occasionally connecting online with their old church during lockdown. When lockdown lifted, their family routine had changed so much the kids didn't want to trek to church on a Sunday anymore. So, they just stopped going altogether.

Claire and Matt aren't real. However, the scenario I describe is one I have seen many times, as people move away and go through different seasons. Someone said to me recently, 'I do have faith in Christ, but it's a personal thing. I don't feel I need to go to church anymore. It's my own private faith.'

In his book *A Churchless Faith*, Alan Jamieson writes about the increasing phenomenon of people, particularly in the Evangelical and Protestant traditions, who leave the Church but still identify as Christians.[1] One of the important lessons to learn from Jamieson's thorough research is that the mainstream Church needs to listen to the experiences of those who have left and to ask – and seek to understand the reasons – why they have done so. This raises a fundamental question for us as we think about being missionary disciples today. How important is the Church bit? How necessary is it that we introduce 'Church' to people? Shouldn't we just seek to draw them to Jesus and the rest can follow?

It was theologian Stanley Hauerwas who said, 'All theology must begin and end with ecclesiology'.[2] What he means is that, in all our thinking about God, we have to include Church somehow. It's not possible to view the Church as an optional extra to the Christian faith. It's there at the beginning and the end.

What is the Church?

As I explained briefly in the introduction, the word 'ecclesiology' comes from the New Testament word *ekklesia*. This roughly translates as 'an assembly of people' and is used in a variety of different ways. In Acts 19:39, it refers to 'a legal assembly', that is, a proper town meeting where grievances could be brought, so in one sense it is not an exclusively 'Christian' word at all.

However, it is an important one to understand if we are going to get our thinking about the Church right.

Generally speaking, the word *ekklesia* is a Greek translation of the Hebrew word *qahal*, so when Jesus (and some of the New Testament writers) use the term *ekklesia*, it carries with it important overtones from its Old Testament usage. In Exodus 19, when God gathers his people at Mount Sinai to establish his covenant with them, God calls them his 'treasured possession' (Exodus 19:5). Out of all the peoples of the world they were special and belonged to him. The assembling of God's people was significant because they did so in the presence of God, hearing from him (Deuteronomy 4:10).

The prophets who came after Moses looked back to this significant time of assembling before God, but they also looked forward to a time of future assembly when all would be gathered (Joel 2:15–16. The idea of gathering together in the presence of God is crucial to the idea of Church, and it is given new meaning by Jesus in his provocative statement, 'For where two or three are gathered in my name, I am there among them' (Matthew 18:20). Church is defined by the presence of the risen Jesus. It doesn't have to be in a particular place or done in a particular way or be of a particular size. As former Archbishop Rowan Williams puts it in the *Mission-Shaped Church* report, 'Church is what happens when people encounter the risen Jesus and deepen that encounter in their encounters with one another.'[3]

Church, then, is all about you, me and Jesus.

However, the reality is that our ideas of Church are governed by our personal preferences – and, dare I say it, even a consumer mentality. We go to a particular church because the worship suits us or we like the preacher. But how do such things sit with a New Testament view of the Church?

Understanding ecclesiology from the New Testament is a bit tricky. You might think there's a particular passage you can go to that gives you a blueprint of how Church should be, but the reality is that it's not that simple. Some people suggest that Acts 2:44–8 presents a pattern for Church, with the disciples meeting in the temple courts, sharing everything in common and breaking bread together. While there are, of course, things we can learn from this early incarnation of church life, it's important to remember that, at this point, there aren't really any Gentiles present, so we can't see it as a perfect blueprint for what is and what isn't Church. Paul gives attention to issues like the order and structure of worship (in response to the apparent chaos reigning in Corinth) and offers some teaching on ministry gifts and the importance of the Lord's Supper, but it's fair to say that detail is somewhat lacking.

In fact, the most common way for the New Testament to talk about the Church is through imagery and pictures.

Images of the Church

Paul Minear's work, *Images of the Church in the New Testament*, states that the New Testament writers use about ninety-six different images when talking about the Church.[4] Minear suggests that images are powerful tools of rhetoric which stir conviction and provoke a response. They are capable of expressing something that cannot be conveyed easily in words. Think for example, of the 'family of God' or 'the body of Christ'.

Some years ago, I attended the funeral of a good friend who had died very young. Her sister described the moment she heard the tragic news by saying, 'It felt as though the whole world had fallen silent.' That image has stayed with me over the years. It describes sudden grief much more powerfully than the words, 'Someone I love has died.' Minear says that images also serve the purpose of directing our actions and priorities as a Church. When a local church selects one image as dominant, it will tend to focus on that over and against others. So, for example, the church that sees itself primarily as the 'family of God' will prize relationships and unity. The church that sees itself as 'salt and light' will tend to focus on distinctive interaction with the world around it. Paul Minear believes that studying the images of the Church in the New Testament is crucial if we are to understand not only what it is, but what it isn't:

> In every generation the use and re-use of the Biblical images has been one path by which the church has tried to learn what the church truly is, so that it can become what it is not. For evoking this kind of self-knowledge, images may be more effective than more formal dogmatic assertions.[5]

Minear suggests that, although these images express different aspects of the Church's corporate life, they are meant to be taken as part of the whole picture and together create a mosaic of what the Church really is.

Some of the images are ones we are well acquainted with, while others will be less familiar. Together they paint a picture of God's purpose and intention for the Church. As we've said, describing the Church in terms of a family (1 Timothy 5:1–2 and Ephesians 3:14–15) emphasises unity and oneness and expresses a sense of nurture and care. The Church as the Bride (Ephesians 5:25–32, 2 Corinthians 11:2) conveys the Church's loving connection to Christ and sense of joyful anticipation. The agricultural images of the vine (John 15:5) and the field (1 Corinthians 3:6–9) communicate the significance of dependence on Christ for our flourishing and fruitfulness. Architectural images, such as the house (Hebrews 3:6), pillar (1 Timothy 3:15) and temple (1 Peter 2:4–8), all point to the importance of Christ as a foundation and our connectedness to him and to one another.

Three dimensions of the Church

If we view these ninety or so different images as pieces of a mosaic, I suggest that, as we step back to take in the whole, three dimensions of the Church stand out. These are what make the Church unique and distinctive from all other human communities. The three dimensions are:

- Vertical – our relationship with Christ
- Horizontal – our relationships with one another
- Cosmic – God's missional purposes for the world

1 Vertical – connected to Christ

The idea of faith apart from community is alien to Christianity. To be born again is to be born into community. Salvation is a work of God's Spirit in which we are simultaneously made new and incorporated into God's family. Becoming a disciple of Jesus, in New Testament terms, has both vertical and horizontal dimensions. You can't have one without the other. This is particularly important for those who have been nurtured in the Evangelical tradition: often an individualistic approach to faith is cultivated – a 'me and my Jesus' or 'me and my Bible' kind of spirituality. If our own individual and personal faith in Christ is strong, we may ask whether we really need the Church and what purpose it serves. I suggest a lack of attention to the ecclesial dimension of our faith is exacerbated in a post-Christian culture, which frequently devalues and misunderstands the role of the Church – except as an occasional nice venue for a special ceremony.

The relegation of faith to the sphere of individual preference and private choice is one of the legacies of the Enlightenment (or modern period). This division between sacred and secular has led to phrases like 'We don't do God', as faith becomes a purely personal affair.[6] It is manifested in the backlash when prominent church leaders 'dare' to interfere in politics. As with the person I mentioned above, many people feel that their Christian faith is private – they believe in God but don't need to go to church to prove it.

Now we must, of course, make a distinction between church as something we do or go to, and Church as something we are. In our Western culture, our identity is often explained in terms of our job or activities. At parties when I am asked, 'What do you do?' explaining that I train clergy for a living is normally either the start of a really interesting conversation or an awkward silence. It may be more helpful to think in terms of Church as something we are, rather than something we do. Our identity as disciples of Jesus is governed by relationality. We are in Christ. As Paul writes to the Ephesians:

> And you also were included in Christ when you heard the message of truth, the gospel of your salvation. When you believed, you were marked in him with a seal, the promised Holy Spirit.
> (Ephesians 1:13, NIVUK)

This idea of being 'in Christ' is of course nurtured by the worshipping life of our Church. Robert Webber describes worship as an 'authentic dialogue between God and God's people'.[7] Worship put on as a programme aims to entertain people, but authentic worship shapes and forms disciples. Webber continues: 'God's presence is made real in the gathering of people, in the preaching of the Word, in the action of the symbols and in the sending forth of the people.'[8]

Becoming a Christian, then, is a supernatural and spiritual act in which we are incorporated into Christ and sealed with the Spirit. This incorporation and sealing, as we shall see, has corporate dimensions too.

2 Horizontal – connected to one another

Probably the most familiar image of the church is the body of Christ, which Paul uses in 1 Corinthians 12. This image demonstrates the interconnectedness of the Church and our dependence upon one another. No part is too small or insignificant; everyone has a role to play, and we are impoverished if a single person is missing. One of the most powerful verses in Paul's description of the body is this, 'If one member suffers, all suffer with it; if one member is honoured, all rejoice together with it' (1 Corinthians 12:26).

The interconnectedness of the body is so complete that when one part experiences pain or hurt, the whole body feels it. As I write this chapter, Christians in Manipur are undergoing horrific violence and persecution. Hundreds of churches have been burned to the ground; many are dead; hundreds are injured and thousands displaced. It is a tragic and terrible situation, but what does it mean for the Church in the West to be 'one body' with the Church in other parts of the world that are facing such turmoil? How can we pray and love and serve in such a way that demonstrates when one suffers, we all suffer together? A phrase you often hear when someone is facing a terrible situation is, 'I can't imagine what you are going through,' but being one body requires that we try our hardest to imagine what it is like. The image of being one body shows that our connection is not about a shared interest – such as a gym club or a pottery class – but a deeper, more visceral bond of shared life together.

The metaphor of the body demonstrates well the distinctiveness of the two dimensions we are talking about here. Each part of the body needs and is connected to every other. Both Colin Gunton and Miroslav Volf have argued that we must understand the Church as integrally linked with the persons of the Trinity.[9] Since

God in his very being is relational, the relationship between the members of the Trinity provides a model of the Church as 'one body' united in relationship with its members. There is distinction in function in the different gifts that the Spirit gives to the Church, but there is an organic unity of purpose and being. The very existence of the Church flows from the Trinitarian community – in one sense, the Trinity is the perfect model for the unity in diversity that we have spoken about. It is a community of self-giving love.

What the body and so many other images of the church profoundly express is the significance of the unity of the church. Unity is a gift of the Spirit as Paul says:

> For in the one Spirit we were all baptised into one body – Jews or Greeks, slaves or free – and we were all made to drink of one Spirit.
> (1 Corinthians 12:13)

The unifying connection between the vertical and horizontal dimensions of the Church is the Holy Spirit who joins together into one body those of different genders, races and ethnicities, making all one in Christ. As New Testament theologian George Eldon Ladd says:

> The *ekklesia* is not to be viewed simply as a human fellowship, bound together by a common religious belief and experience. It is this, but it is more than this: it is the creation of God through the Holy Spirit. Therefore there is and can properly be only one *ekklesia*.[10]

The Church as the creation of God by the gift of the Spirit is most clearly demonstrated at Pentecost. As the disciples receive the Holy Spirit, they begin to proclaim the good news of Jesus to those who have travelled into Jerusalem from far and wide. People are able to hear the good news in languages familiar to them, and we read that 'that day about three thousand persons were added' (Acts 2:41). The phenomenon of glossolalia (speaking in tongues) demonstrates a key principle at the heart of the horizontal dimension of church – unity within diversity. Ladd comments:

> The Pentecostal tongues have a symbolic significance, and suggest that this new event in redemptive history is designed for the whole world and would unite people of diverse tongues in a new unity of the *ekklesia*.[11]

There were both inclusive and exclusive elements to belonging to this new community, or *ekklesia*. All were welcome, whatever their social status, ethnicity or gender. However, incorporation into this new community also involved a radical turning away from your previous way of life and sense of identity. Not optional but integral, it brought you into relationship with those who were different to you, sometimes in every way imaginable.

One way in which the horizontal dimension of the Church's life is enacted is through the vital principle of 'unity in diversity'. Newbigin remarks that while there were many different religions offering salvation in the Graeco-Roman period of the first century, only Christianity offered the *ekklesia*, an assembly for all. Paul's letters frequently address the remarkable cross-societal communities that are gathered together in churches throughout the ancient world. In 1 Corinthians, he states that 'not many of you were wise by human standards, not many were powerful, not many were of noble birth' (1:26), clearly implying that some were. The idea that those of noble birth might mix in community with those who were not was utterly revolutionary. In the same way, Galatians expresses the ground-breaking reality of a community where all are equal and identified collectively as children of God: 'There is neither Jew nor Gentile, neither slave nor free, nor is there male and female, for you are all one in Christ Jesus' (Galatians 3:28, NIVUK).

In a society where divisions across gender, social status and ethnicities ran deep, it is hard to underestimate the impact of a Church that extended beyond such fractures. Wayne Meeks in *The First Urban Christians* suggests that the question of social status was rigid and divisive, and the Church's revolutionary way of bringing those with very little financial status together with wealthier members of society was a relief to both groups, for whom loneliness and societal alienation was challenging.[12] Meeks further suggests that the Roman Empire contained the perfect conditions for the early church to thrive. As the gospel was good news for all, it brought together those who needed help and those with resources at their disposal. Meeks asks the question:

> Would, then, the intimacy of Christian groups become a welcome refuge, the emotion-charged language of family and affection and the image of a caring, personal God powerful antidotes, while the master symbol of the crucified saviour crystallised a believable picture of the way the world seemed really to work?[13]

The horizontal dimension of the Church is a supernatural gift of the Spirit, drawing people from different walks of life, ethnicities and social statuses together into one community. Such community is based on a stronger connection than simply having 'things in common': it is a spiritual demonstration of the power of God in bringing together what was previously divided. Throughout the book of Acts, it is the Holy Spirit who is constantly pushing the Church into new and more diverse territory, crossing boundaries of culture and race. This is most powerfully illustrated in the meeting of Peter and Cornelius in Acts 10. Peter is sent by God (through a miraculous and rather strange vision) to the house of a Gentile centurion. According to the social systems of the day, these two should not meet, and yet Acts records the most profound encounter of both vertical and horizontal dimensions. To the complete surprise of Peter and his companions, the Spirit falls onto the Gentile and his family, without Peter having to do anything. It is a remarkable demonstration of the Spirit going beyond the limited possibilities of our imagination. It is a landmark moment in the history of the Church. As the following chapters in Acts show, Peter tries to make sense of what he has experienced and attempts to convince those who had not been present that what happened was the purest and most perfect expression of the gospel. For those who were troubled by this unusual and forbidden boundary-crossing, Peter finds a rationale in the experience of the Spirit, stating simply, 'If then God gave them the same gift that he gave us when we believed in the Lord Jesus Christ, who was I that I could hinder God?' (Acts 11:17). It is the Spirit of God that transcends human, societal and religious differences. Willie James Jennings encapsulates the significance of the moment beautifully:

> In a quiet corner of the Roman Empire, in the home of a centurion, a rip in the fabric of space and time has occurred. All those who would worship Jesus may enter a new vision of intimate space and a new time that will open up endless new possibilities of life with others.[14]

This idea of the 'rip in the fabric of space and time' leads us to think about the third (and often neglected) dimension of the Church – the cosmic.

3 Cosmic – called to the world

The letter to the Ephesians looks at the Church, not primarily from a practical perspective, but from a cosmic one. Its opening chapter positions Christ on a cosmic scale, as the one in whom and through whom all things are redeemed and reconciled. It's like the opposite of the *Wizard of Oz* moment when Dorothy peeks behind the curtain and discovers the wizard is just an ordinary man using props and trickery to feign greatness. In Ephesians, we peek behind the curtain of human affairs and see a cosmic Christ who is indeed all great and all powerful. The letter shows the cosmic dimensions of our human interactions.

Paul uses a number of images of the Church in this letter to make clear his point that God's work of salvation in Christ results in a new community in which Jews and Gentiles come together. In many ways, Paul is doing the theological work of explaining the significance of Cornelius and Peter meeting in Acts 10, using the image of the body (Ephesians 2:16), the household (2:19) and the family (3:15). It is particularly interesting that Paul is quick to note that what is significant about the Church as one body is that it is a new creation. It is not the case that Jewish Christians have made concessions and allowed Gentiles to belong. A community where Jew and Gentile belong together is a spiritual work of new creation, unlike anything else that exists in the entire universe:

> For he is our peace; in his flesh he has made both groups into one and has broken down the dividing wall, that is, the hostility between us. He has abolished the law with its commandments and ordinances, so that he might create in himself one new humanity in place of the two, thus making peace, and might reconcile both groups to God in one body through the cross, thus putting to death that hostility through it. So he came and proclaimed peace to you who were far off and peace to those who were near; for through him both of us have access in one Spirit to the Father.
> (Ephesians 2:14–18)

In our day-to-day efforts to pursue unity, we can so easily lose sight of this reality. When consumerism seeps into our churches, we become accustomed to thinking of Church in terms of what we like or what suits us. Paul here reminds us that Church isn't meant to be easy. It is spectacularly ambitious in its endeavour to bring together those who are so different that our very existence in the world can make us hostile to one another. Unity isn't primarily about making concessions to allow the other to coexist. Unity here is about a completely miraculous work of the Spirit to create a new humanity, a body of people who are recipients of Christ's peace and the gift of the Spirit, and so live in unity with one another. And it gets even more exciting... Paul claims this in the following chapter, 'so that through the church, the wisdom of God in its rich variety might now be made known to the rulers and authorities in the heavenly places' (Ephesians 3:10).

In the creation of this new body, 'the wisdom of God in its rich variety' is made known, Paul says. In other words, God is shown to be all good and all wise: God's character and beauty is demonstrated. But to whom? To the 'rulers and authorities in the heavenly places'. This phrase is used later in Ephesians 6:12, when Paul talks about the spiritual battle that all Christians face. The rulers and authorities are those evil and demonic spirits that scheme against Christ and the Church. In other words, Paul is saying that when those divided in our world today come together in Christ, it declares God's goodness and wisdom in the cosmic realm. Unity here is not pitched as 'you'd better stick together as there's not many of you now', but 'you'd better stick together because Satan trembles when you do.' If that doesn't get us out of bed in the morning and onto our knees to pray for the church down the road, I don't know what will.

This idea of the Church revealing the wisdom and goodness of God is one that has resonated with me for some time. In fact, when I was ordained, my friend Emma made me a piece of artwork based on Ephesians 3:10, and it sits proudly in my office. It is a reminder of the bigger picture behind the often mundane and challenging difficulties of unity in practice: the little decisions to consider others, to stick together despite the challenges. The reminder of the cosmic purpose is a powerful motivation.

However, the idea of the Church displaying and declaring things in the heavenly realms also points towards something important about the purpose of the Church in the world today. At the Last Supper, Jesus says these poignant words to his disciples: 'I give you a new commandment, that you love one another. Just as I have loved you, you also should love one another. By this everyone will know that you are my disciples, if you have love for one another' (John 13:34–5).

Jesus hints here at the new body that will be brought to life by the initiation and gift of the Spirit. He shows that love will be the way and rule of this new community. And then, in the words, 'by this everyone will know', he shows the outworking of love in community. Through genuine, authentic and deep-seated love for one another, the Church will influence the world. Through love lived out in sacrificial, practical and thoughtful ways, the Church will be known as belonging to Jesus.

So, the vertical and horizontal dimensions of the Church (our relationships with Christ and to one another) take on significance both in cosmic terms – declaring the wisdom of God in the heavenly realms – and in local communities and in the public sphere, as they point to the abundant love and grace of God in Christ.

Four principles for practice

Let's now explore what this might look in practice through considering four principles.

1 View community as a gift

The 'third dimension' of the Church has alerted us to the reality of the Church's purpose beyond its own existence. We know its goal is never purely our own good feeling and sense of community, for we're aware of the constant, outward momentum of a missionary God who longs to draw in all people. Church is both a demonstration of God's goodness and an invitation to be incorporated within a community of divine love. If Church is our encounter with the risen Jesus, deepened by our encounter with others, then love becomes both the demonstration of that and the means of invitation. It is an act of love to welcome others into such a community. We thought earlier about how we tend to think of mission and evangelism in individualistic terms, the goal being for someone to pray the prayer and become a Christian. However, what we actually have to offer people is that and so much more: it is an invitation into a community like no other. It is not enough that we serve the world and do things for others, as good and as important as that is; we are also called to offer people what lies at the heart of the Church's existence: community with Christ. In this way, Church in the everyday is both a sign pointing to God's love and a portal by which people are invited to know God's love for themselves.

In a world that is marred by discord, a community where all can belong and find their place is a powerful apologetic. Jon Yates vigorously addresses the increasing divisions we experience in his book *Fractured*:

> Our problem is not that we are different from each other. People have always lived with difference. There has never been a country on earth where everyone thought the same, believed the same, looked the same and sounded the same. No, the problem is not that we are different from each other; it is that we are distant from 'the other'. The problem is our lack of interaction with those who are different; that we live in social bubbles filled with people 'just like me'.[15]

The Church is uniquely positioned to provide a space in which we can and should encounter those who are different from us. As we've seen, the heart of the New Testament idea of Church is a unified community in which those who look, think and are different come together. A survey by the insurance company Aviva discovered that 1 in 10 people (that's over 5 million in the UK today) don't know the name of their next-door neighbour.[16] The Covid pandemic sadly got us used to the idea of social distancing, keeping others at bay, surrounding ourselves with a select group of six. Now the pandemic is well in the past, do we continue to socially distance ourselves from others in our neighbourhood? Does the idea that the Church might be a gathering point for the local community seem woefully idealistic? The truth is, that a Church that draws people together from all walks of life can be a gift to the world. A non-church friend once told me that, though she couldn't get her head around the idea of God, she envied my being part of an intergenerational multi-ethnic community.

Theologian Harvey Kwiyani writes robustly on issues of multiculturalism and race in the Church today. He points to the positive impact that (particularly African) migration has had on the Church in the UK but suggests that Sunday mornings continue to be one of the most segregated times for Christians here.[17] The sad reality is that, rather than providing a glorious alternative, the Church can perpetuate the social bubbles that exist in other spheres of life. We need to recapture the sense of the Church as a gift to the world, a place where all can belong and find a home, a place where everybody knows your name. This gift is good news for us as individuals, drawing us into a physical community, when so much of our time is spent online through various apps and social media channels. This is not to deny that, for some, online church has been and continues to be an expression of inclusion and belonging, where those who are house-bound or unable to physically attend church can find a welcoming and supportive community.

This gift of Church is also good news for our world, enabling us to bridge some of the divides that Jon Yates addresses, such as not knowing people who vote differently to us or look and sound different. Of course, while we assume the gift of community is about Sundays, there are seven days a week during which the Church can be a gift to the world.

Belinda is a fitness instructor in Essex, having built up a successful business running keep fit and pilates classes. During lockdown, a space became available in the church where she worships, and she moved her business across there. Every Saturday, the church ran a café in the church foyer, and the church hall was rented out for regular dance classes and other groups. Belinda noticed there was no interaction between the two. She had the idea of welcoming the parents who were waiting for their children into the café for coffee and a piece of cake. The café began to bustle with activity, and Belinda got to know those coming. She decided to start a 'knit and natter group' so people could learn new creative skills and enjoy chatting as they crocheted and knitted. One lady who joined suggested that they make blankets for the local hospice. The group, a mix of those who went to church and those who did not, worked together on these blankets, weaving colours and threads together as they shared their lives and producing beautifully crocheted blankets for people in their last hours. One particular member of the group, who was going through a difficult time and on a long waiting list to get support, was greatly helped by the compassion and kindness of the others who attended.

Parents began to take drinks from the café in with them as they went to watch the dance class, while others stopped to chat to volunteers. Friendships were formed, and over time some parents would request prayer for a particular circumstance they were facing. Having the volunteers ask the next week how they were getting on touched people. Belinda found out that some of the dads who attended the community were into Warhammer, so they started a Warhammer group with (mostly!) men, creating and playing together. Someone donated thousands of pounds worth of LEGO to the church, so a local congregation member who loved LEGO was persuaded to start a LEGO club, which proved hugely popular with the children. In time, the double doors to the church on the other side of the foyer were opened up so that the LEGO and Warhammer clubs could have more space. Each week, the LEGO club would focus on a different theme and the children would be set a challenge to create the tallest tower, best boat and so on. One week, the club was invited to Messy Church to share their LEGO-builds as part of the creative worship. In short, opening up the café space attracted all sorts of people from different walks of life with different interests. Belinda has seen some come to faith and some begin to attend church, while others have simply enjoyed experiencing the gift of Church in the community.

2 Practice hospitality

If the Church is a gift to be given to the world, then generosity needs to be at the heart of church life. Christopher James conducted some research among church plants in Seattle, arguably one of the most secular cities in the US and, in that respect, like many British cities.[18] James found that across a variety of different models and styles of church planting, there were five common features in church plants that were flourishing and growing. One of these was the practice of hospitality. Every plant in Seattle that had experienced growth and stability had prioritised hospitality as a foundational principle. James says this:

Hospitality disciplines mission to take shape as a simultaneous proactive and noncoercive activity. The spirituality that naturally accompanies a robust practice of hospitality is one that seeks God in the midst of the other and the ordinary. The forms of ecclesial identity born of hospitable practice locate the church in its proper solidarity with the world and its diversity without collapsing the church into the world. Far from being a strategic mission gimmick, hospitality orients missional ecclesiopraxis.[19]

Hospitality, according to James, is not a missional strategy to get people into church – 'give them lovely food and perhaps they'll agree to attend' – but a manifestation of the church's presence in the world. Missionally speaking, it is relational rather than about an exchange of goods. Theologian Cathy Ross agrees with James saying, 'Hospitality is in itself a prophetic practice as it crosses boundaries, welcomes all and involves taking risks.'[20]

We are familiar with the concept of hospitality as something we give or do to others. During my early involvement with All Saints, I remember one Sunday morning a lady sharing in the service how she was struggling financially, couldn't find any work and didn't have enough to keep her and her toddler in their rented accommodation. The church pulled together, praying for her and offering what they could. By the evening service, the vicar had to ask people to stop giving money as she had received way in excess of what she needed. Such can be the generosity of God's people when church becomes family. We'd probably associate this with social action or what Paul Keeble calls a 'mission-to' approach.[21] However, while hospitality is a powerful expression of Christian mission, it cannot be the whole picture. Christian hospitality requires the Church to be both host and guest. It is not a one-way street.

Sharing meals was central to the ministry of Jesus. In a culture where mealtimes were governed by rules of separation (who you ate with) and cleanliness (what and how you ate), Jesus' approach is entirely boundary-crossing and revolutionary, epitomised in this famous passage:

And as he sat at dinner in Levi's house, many tax-collectors and sinners were also sitting with Jesus and his disciples – for there were many who followed him. When the scribes of the Pharisees saw that he was eating with sinners and tax-collectors, they said to his disciples, 'Why does he eat with tax-collectors and sinners?' When Jesus heard this, he said to them, 'Those who are well have no need of a physician, but those who are sick; I have come to call not the righteous but sinners.'
(Mark 2:15–17)

Isn't it remarkable that Jesus simply having a meal with people is a topic for discussion? His radical welcome is demonstrated in his choice of dinner location, while his choice of guests arouses the suspicion of those who presumably think he should be dining with more worthy folk. In fact, as William Lane points out, that term 'sinners' was a technical one used by the Pharisees to denote those who had no interest in the Pharisaic standards of the ceremonial cleanliness required at such meals.[22]

Jesus sharing meals with people is something that occurs repeatedly throughout the Gospels, and it's interesting to note that on this occasion, as on countless others, he finds himself as the guest rather than the host. Positioning ourselves as the guest is a powerful way for the Church in the West to recognise its marginal status. It is not simply the case that we need strangers as an outlet for our love; strangers allow us to learn and grow and see ourselves differently.

Creating spaces where genuine hospitality, meal-sharing and boundary-crossing can take place is part of the Church's gift to the world. At the heart of this vision of Christian hospitality is a willingness to spend time in the presence of others. It seems these days we are always in a rush. Productivity apps coach us in how to make the most of every second of the day, and we need mindfulness apps to encourage us to take our time to slow down and eat. We are always rushing on to the next thing. Only 28% of families eat together, Sainsbury's found in a recent survey.[23]

It is because it takes time that giving and receiving hospitality is a prophetic statement of the importance of the other in our increasingly frenetic, consumeristic world. The year we spent Christmas in Uganda was one of the most significant experiences of hospitality and the gift of time I have ever experienced. It was our first time away from home and family for Christmas, and at the ages of three, eight and eleven, we wondered how our boys would cope without all the usual (let's be honest here) consumerism. We had been invited to spend Christmas evening with a Ugandan family who have become very dear to us. There were about twenty people present, and the meal lasted several hours, as we savoured chicken stew, chapatis cooked over the outdoor fire and matooke, steamed in vibrant green leaves. Each of us had been encouraged to buy one present for one other person (aka Secret Santa) and when we got to the gift-giving 'ceremony' (as I later realised it was), instead of placing our gifts in the middle and all opening them together, one person presented their gift to another, doing a dance and singing a song on the way. Each of us opened our present in sheer delight, to the cheers and clapping of those present. It took hours, but it felt like a slow explosion of joy into our lives. As my boys unwrapped their gifts – bright hats woven out of banana leaves – they too squealed with delight and joined in the singing and dancing as they offered their presents to their new friends, who were rapidly becoming family. At every Christmas since, we have reminisced about the slow, generous simplicity of our Ugandan Christmas. It remains our favourite family Christmas of all time.

Hospitality, where we both give and receive, is one of the most precious gifts the Church has to offer the world. In a world of increasing fear of the other, where racial tensions around migration run high, creating spaces where friendships across boundaries can flourish might be one of the most powerful missional tasks of the Church. Such friendships can form in your own home, in the homes of others, in local community spaces like libraries, sports clubs and volunteer organisations, or in a church-facilitated space like Belinda's café church. Hospitality allows strangers to become friends and friends to become like family. Mission like this is not an exchange of goods, a service done to another, or the passing on of vital information, but a life shared: 'So deeply do we care for you that we are determined to share with you not only the gospel of God but also our own selves, because you have become very dear to us' (1 Thessalonians 2:8).

3 Cherish diversity

The issue of hospitality naturally raises the question of diversity: who are we being hospitable to and from whom are we receiving hospitality? Christian hospitality will always be defined by boundary-crossing friendships. One of the most interesting books I read on mission this year was *Unlikely Friends*, which talks of the history of mission through the small, often untold stories of boundary-crossing, genuine friendships. Friendships which span cultural, racial and societal differences are not a strategy for mission, they are a foundational practice for the missional church.

> In a context of ongoing global inequality, small gestures of sharing meals, learning to appreciate new foods, and claiming 'others' as friends can subtly but profoundly reshape the political and economic order, contributing to the formation of a global church whose members' allegiance to each other surpasses their commitment to nationalist imaginations and global systems of domination.[24]

In our post-Brexit Western context, where societal division seems more apparent than ever, the importance of friendship in crossing cultural and ethnic barriers cannot be underestimated and carries a prophetic and eschatological power. Friendships which transcend barriers of disability or neurodivergence speak powerfully of God's new society, where all are valued and all have something to contribute and offer.

Earlier this year, as I prepared for a reflective service on Maundy Thursday, I was stunned by the power of Jesus' prayers on his last night. Of all the things he could have focused on, I was struck by his prayer for the future Church, for you and me. The consistent theme that weaves through is one of unity: 'that all of them may be one, Father, just as you are in me and I am in you' (John 17:21, NIVUK). The most powerful apologetic of the gospel is a community that authentically and generously lives out the good news in unity and diversity. This should not mean seeking to minimise difference but rather celebrating and cherishing it. Kwiyani comments:

> Being in the kingdom of God does not erase our cultural differences. To do so would be colonialism, and God does not colonize. Instead, the kingdom of God encourages all cultures to coexist whilst challenging them all (often through their intercultural encounters) to measure up to the image of the Son of God. The kingdom of God finds its fullest expression in intercultural mutuality. It is a multicultural kingdom.[25]

In chapter 3 we considered the Church Growth Movement and its impact on our ideas of success and failure in the Church. One of the principles at the heart of that approach which has shaped some of our ideas of planting and mission is the homogenous unit principle.

Donald McGavran was a third-generation missionary and missiologist in India who grew discouraged by the lack of people coming to faith, despite huge missionary efforts. McGavran observed that Western missionaries were preoccupied with individuals praying the sinner's prayer and so being converted.[26] He began to question what it might mean to see a transformation of whole people groups in a way that preserved indigenous identity and sought a 'Christward movement' in an entire social grouping. In one sense, McGavran's approach positively seeks to cherish people's inherited and indigenous cultures. However, it was later developed into the 'the homogenous unit principle', which suggests that people are more likely to become Christians if they don't have to cross any racial, linguistic or social barriers. While there is a genuine challenge here for the Church in terms of its willingness to learn the languages of others and incarnate itself into the diverse cultures of the Western world, this principle can be used to give licence for planting and pioneering that doesn't draw diverse people into unity and doesn't challenge the separations which divide our society. As theologian Miroslav Volf comments:

> Our coziness with the surrounding culture has made us so blind to many of its evils that, instead of calling them into question, we offer our own versions of them – in God's name and with a good conscience. Those who refuse to be party to our mimicry we brand sectarians.[27]

When the Western churches remain monoculturally homogenous, do we reflect the individualistic and consumeristic culture of a post-Brexit Britain rather than acting as a flashforward of the heavenly community to come (Revelation 7:9)? Tom Greggs goes so far as to say that we need one another to prevent the Church from its sinful tendency to turn in on itself. We need one another, in all our glorious difference, to enable God's Church be all it is meant to be:

> Variety and difference in the life of the church is crucial since the otherness of these others is a divine reality given to the believer in the life of the church to orientate her away from her fallen and individualized, self-orientated identity and outwards towards the ways of divine grace. The community needs to be a community in which there is variance between individual members such that the believer is enabled genuinely to be turned outwards to other humans.[28]

The Pauline vision of unity in the Spirit is not about obliterating differences but celebrating and cherishing them. A nice ideal, maybe, but how do we live this in practice? I want to suggest three initial, simple steps. The first is that we *look*. Look around at your church. And then look at your local community. Who is in the community but not the church? Who is missing from your church? We need to pay heed to the places of influence in our church. Who leads from the front? Who gets to speak, to pray?

Who is working behind the scenes in the background? Are they being noticed? The first stage is simply opening our eyes, so we are aware of the reality of our churches and where imbalances or gaping holes are present.

The second stage is *listening or learning*. Genuine friendship requires us to listen to one another and learn from one another's experiences. The most important listening is done in relationship. Through creating those hospitality spaces where genuine, boundary-crossing friendships can form, we can learn to listen to one another, to hear the pain of exclusion and racism, and to be changed by our interaction with others. It is perhaps no surprise then, that my faith has been impacted most remarkably by Christians from different parts of the global church, whether through spending time in churches in Argentina, Uganda or Spain or through friends on my doorstep in London. I will always be thankful for a dear friend Winnie who introduced me to the work of Afua Kuma, a Ghanian midwife, who writes grass roots theology about Jesus in ways that have stretched and enriched my own understanding. We can also listen and learn through books, and a great starting point for those wanting to explore issues of race in the British church would be Ben Lindsay's excellent *We Need to Talk about Race* and Harvey Kwiyani's *Multicultural Kingdom*.[29] Both these books give a penetrating analysis of the reasons for the lack of racial diversity in our churches and offer helpful ways forward.

The third stage is that of *loving*. Listening is important, but loving is crucial and as we have already been reminded, love is a verb. It drives us to act and to do. Listening and learning means that we need to be active in our pursuit of racial justice, seeking to uproot the ugly stain of racism wherever we find it, in our own personal lives or in our churches. Loving our sisters and brothers means that pursuing justice has to be at the heart of what it is to be a missionary disciple. Loving one another means that we will not just 'put up with' diversity, but will actively seek, cherish and celebrate it. We may look at our churches and think they seem relatively diverse, but who is conceding to whom? Are those in the minority simply expected to secede to the majority culture? Is different cultural expression allowed in the side room but not centre stage? We are not seeking here a lowest common denominator where everyone is happy with everything, but rather a community which celebrates and champions one another's differences, allowing each to shine, as collectively we make manifest the glorious body of Christ. On a micro level this will compel us to ask difficult and uncomfortable questions about everything from our Sunday services to our discipleship programmes, from our leadership structures to our hospitality. It will undoubtedly involve us taking a hard look at the role of power in our churches. It is all too easy to seek a veneer of diversity while still prioritising and trusting those like me. Kwiyani is quick to point out that the future of the Church in the West might depend upon this very issue of learning to listen, love and work in partnership together. The task which faces the Church in the West is a daunting one. Perhaps, as Volf suggests, the answer is on our doorstep:

> In order to keep our allegiance to Jesus Christ pure, we need to nurture commitment to the multicultural community of Christian churches. We need to see ourselves and our own understanding of God's future with the eyes of Christians from other cultures, listen to voices of Christians from other cultures so as to make sure that the voice of our culture has not drowned out the voice of Jesus Christ, 'the one Word of God'.[30]

When Peter visited Cornelius, he discovered the power of encounter with someone who was different. We can't contemplate the present existence of the Church without this exchange. And yet, neither can we contemplate its future existence without the replication of that moment in countless communities and places throughout the world.

4 See the bigger picture

Our final principle for practice is the reminder that as disciples of Jesus we are part of a community which stretches across the world.

We are connected members of one global family. Paul writes that all were baptised into one body. This sense of oneness was lived out on both a micro and macro level. For example, the church in Corinth knew that it was called to be one body across the divides of Corinthian culture, but it also had a sense of being connected to other churches through the Apostle Paul's ministry. In the Nicene Creed, we say that we are part of the one, holy, catholic and apostolic Church. When we talk about being part of the 'catholic' Church, that is not referring to a particular denomination (such as Roman Catholic) but stating that we are part of a universal Christian community. At the centre of that statement is the belief that we are not on our own but are connected to the entire global Church throughout the world, and throughout all time. As Volf says:

> Every local church is a catholic community because, in a profound sense, all other churches are a part of that church, all of them shape – or ought to shape – its identity. As all churches together form a worldwide ecumenical community, so each church in a given culture is a catholic community. Each church must therefore say, 'I am not only I; all other churches, rooted in diverse cultures, are part of me too.' Each needs all to be properly itself.[31]

The Church in Acts lived out this sense of being one part of a bigger whole through their financial support of one another. In Acts 11:29, we hear of the church in Judea having a difficult time and the church in Jerusalem sending both financial aid and people to encourage and support it. It's tempting to skip over the endings of Paul's letters because they tend to contain lists of people we don't know, but so often those names are an expression of one Church, connected in Christ, through different locations. People were being sent to encourage and serve one another.

One of the things I learned early on in our time in Uganda, when I found myself in front of a church of several thousand without any warning and encouraged to 'bring greetings', was that I was required to share good wishes from my home church in Peckham. I was to say hello and we love you on behalf of people they had never met, and would probably never meet, but with whom they celebrate a special bond in Christ. When we returned from Uganda, I was most excited to bring greetings back to our London church from the many churches we had visited. This led to a slightly more joyful jumping element in the service than most were used to! But it conveyed powerfully that we are all one in Christ. Many of us will have mission partners in other parts of the world: allowing space in our services to hear from them and experience church in a different way is a crucial part of recognising we are all one Church. There is so much we can and should do to encourage and support the global church.

However, our connection with the global church isn't just about fostering partnerships overseas but also about who is on our doorstep. In reflecting on the missional challenge of the minority church in the West, theologian Stefan Paas is quick to point out that partnership is the only way to guard against competition which is ultimately harmful for the Church.[32] We need to be willing to partner with other churches in our local area or, at the very least, to know what they are doing and pray for them. It is arrogant and presumptive to assume that our church is the only one our local area needs, though this way of thinking is a very real temptation to a successful and growing church. Instead, we need to look for where there are others we can bless with resources, or where there might be potential to join in partnership with others. One of my favourite sermons by John Wesley is entitled the 'Catholic Spirit'. In it he acknowledges differences across denominations and yet recognises the magnitude of the missional task (he was of course concerned for the conversion of the country to Christ). He suggests that this goal will be served by unity and a willingness to reach beyond the divides. I will end this chapter with his words as he preaches on 2 Kings 10:15:

'If thine heart be right, as mine with thy heart,' then love me with a very tender affection, as a friend that is closer than a brother (sic); as a brother in Christ, a fellow citizen of the New Jerusalem, a fellow soldier engaged in the same warfare under the same captain of our salvation. Love me as a companion in the kingdom and patience of Jesus, and a joint heir of his glory.[33]

Discussion

1 Which image of the Church do you most resonate with and why? (It could be body, bride, temple, etc.)
2 In what ways can you cherish and celebrate diversity in your church? What are the challenges it brings and how can you address them?
3 Who is present in your local community but not in your church? How might you try to reach out to them? What changes might your church need to make to become more accessible and welcoming to them?

5
Church as witness: Living the gospel story

In the spring of 2018, I visited Iona for the first time. We were staying on the mainland, so it took some time to get there – embarking on the car ferry to Mull, driving across the stunning scenery and then taking a smaller ferry to the island of Iona. It is small – only about one mile wide and four miles long – so you can easily walk the length of it. To the north, sits the monastery with its beautiful Celtic stonework and stunning views across the Scottish Hebrides. Iona is believed to be a 'thin' place, one of those special locations where God's presence seems almost tangible. The day I visited was gloriously sunny, and I felt incredibly moved to pray where Christian people had gathered to pray for over 1,500 years, in a place that played a significant role in the conversion of the North of England.

Columba was a strong and apostolic leader who travelled from Ireland in AD 563 along with a team of twelve. He set to work building a monastery on the island from wood and clay. Over the centuries, the monastery housed a scriptorium in which some of the finest illuminated manuscripts of the Bible were created, possibly even the beautiful Book of Kells. Iona became a starting point for the Celtic mission through Scotland, which eventually spread through Columba's successor St Aidan to Lindisfarne in the north of England and then to the Anglo-Saxon south.

In his book *Recovering the Past: Celtic and Roman Mission,* John Finney contrasts the Roman way of mission with the Celtic one.[1] The Roman model was built on the idea of presenting the Christian message, and someone then deciding to respond to Christ and being given an invitation to church. It is not hard to see ways in which this model has influenced many of our Western approaches to evangelism, particularly the large stadium outreaches in which the preacher calls for an immediate response. By contrast, Finney suggests, the Celtic model of mission was to establish a community and invite people to join, to allow space for them to explore faith and then offer an invitation to follow Jesus. This might also be described as a 'belonging before believing' approach. Arguably, such a model of community-first evangelism was hugely successful in the Celtic mission among the pagan Scots and Anglo-Saxons. Finney questions whether, in our increasingly secular society, the Celtic model might hold some wisdom for us. From his rocky outpost in the Scottish Hebrides, Columba led a network of Christian communities which both embodied and narrated the Christian gospel of hope in Christ. Members worshipped, prayed and shared meals together, welcomed the poor and served those locally who were in need. For Columba and his companions, there was no sense of the gospel message apart from the community that lives it. Newbigin comments on this idea too:

> The business of the church is to tell and embody a story, the story of God's mighty acts in creation and redemption and of God's promises concerning what will be in the end. The church affirms the truth of this story by celebrating it, interpreting it, and enacting it in the life of the contemporary world. It has no other way of affirming its truth ... The church's affirmation is that the story that it tells, embodies and enacts is the true story and that others are to be evaluated by reference to it.[2]

Living the gospel story

New Testament scholar Kavin Rowe has studied the book of Acts intensively and has come to the conclusion that the word *ekklesia* (which we saw earlier meant 'assembly') is not about the particulars of church; rather, the book of Acts is concerned with how the early Christian community shows what 'witness to the Lord Jesus

Christ in a world that did not know him' looks like in practice.[3] Instead of presenting us with a blueprint for Church, the book of Acts demonstrates the impact that growing authentic Christian communities had on the ancient world. To live as a Christian involved a completely new way of being, both in allegiance to Christ and in relationship to God's family, the Church. Living this way was radical and distinctive, and impacted the first disciples' private and public lives. It was both radically inclusive – everyone was welcome – but also essentially exclusive – you had to renounce your former way of life in order to follow Jesus. The first *ekklesia* turned the world of the first century upside down:

> If we wish to talk about ecclesiology, according to Acts, we must talk primarily about a theologically explicated habit of being that is noticeably different from the larger practices and assumptions that shape daily life in the Greco-Roman world. According to Acts, ecclesiology is simply the communal form of life that is living in obedience to the Lord of all; it is a form of life that is at once political and theological, or public and private, or, to say it only slightly differently, all-encompassing.[4]

A common way of thinking about the Church in such terms has been to talk about the Church as a 'herald' of the divine word. This is a feature of Protestant ecclesiology in particular, and is associated with the theologian Karl Barth, although you can trace its origin to the Reformers (Luther and Calvin). The model is that of John the Baptist, the great herald of the gospel, who points to Jesus in word and deed. In the same way, the Church through its life and words points towards Jesus. It is not only that the Church is *made up of* evangelists and witnesses, but the Church itself *is* both evangelist and witness to the gospel of Jesus.

This means that the Christian Church is all about the gospel of Jesus Christ – it is a gospel community. The word 'gospel' in the New Testament is *evangelion*, which when translated means 'good news'. It is obviously the root from which we get all the words connected with 'evangelism'. The church is a community formed because there is good news from God. It is the community that is both to embody (in its worship and action) and proclaim the *evangelion* to the world. As Baptist theologian John Colwell puts it:

The gospel story defines the life of the Christian and the life of the Church, while the life of the Church and the life of the Christian is, correspondingly, a retelling and reinterpreting of that gospel story. The world has no access to the gospel story other than as it is narrated in the life, worship, and proclamation of the Church … Through its service and being as witness, the Church is a rendering of the gospel to the world.[5]

Being a gospel community

There are three aspects of the gospel that will help us think about how the Church shapes its identity and purpose in the light of it.

1 The gospel as public truth

Our tendency when we think about evangelism is to assume it is always individualistic, one person to another. However, the gospel isn't just truth for individuals, it is also public truth, and it shapes the world we find ourselves in. It is public truth for every epoch of time, culture and society. Okesseon expresses this in the following way:

Developing a public missiology is also critical for those of us living in the West, where complex forms of racism, poverty, human trafficking, sexism, and the intermingling of economic and political ideologies with religious resource daily vexes public life. We have been trained to witness to individuals but not to the complex publics that spin, turn, and merge together as if participating in some large ballroom dance.[6]

As we saw in chapter 1, the people of Israel were called to live out their communal life with God in public. It was to impact and 'bless' those around them. In a similar way, we saw in chapter 3 that the Thessalonian church was praised for the way in which the message of the gospel 'rang out' (1 Thessalonians 1:8, NIVUK). They were known publicly as being people of faith, love and hope. The Church's calling as a witness to the gospel is to point to – and also to demonstrate – an alternative way of being. As Okesson suggests, 'Public theologians believe that we love society best by critiquing it, calling it back to God's created purposes.'[7]

Acknowledging that the gospel is public truth means that the Church cannot stay silent on issues of injustice and sin.

When my children were younger, I used to love taking them to Battersea Park Zoo. Their favourite thing to visit every time was the meerkats. There was an underground tunnel you could climb through before popping up in a Perspex dome in the middle of the meerkats' enclosure. Meerkats are known and loved for their endearing ability to stand on their hind legs, perfectly upright, as they scan the surrounding area for any impending danger. I always find it a bit sad to see them doing that in a south London zoo, rather than the African Savannah, where the presence of an over exuberant five-year-old behind glass is rather less dangerous than a martial eagle, poised to swoop down and carry off its prey. However, despite the security of its surroundings, the humble meerkat remains constantly alert, always on guard, ready for any eventuality.

'Being alert' is a helpful image for thinking about the public witness of the Church. In the Old Testament, the prophets are sometimes described as 'lookouts' or 'sentinels' who stand on a high place keeping watch (Isaiah 21:6 and Ezekiel 3:17). Unlike the military watch person who would scan the surrounding area for impending physical attack by the enemy, the prophets were to stand on the lookout and to speak about and for God.

In Luke 4, Jesus enters the synagogue in his home town and startles those present by reading from Isaiah 63 on the Old Testament scroll. What is surprising is not that Jesus reads the passage – that would have been the expected behaviour of a Jewish rabbi – but his conclusion that, 'Today this scripture has been fulfilled in your hearing' (Luke 4:21). Let's look at what Jesus says is being fulfilled through his person and ministry:

The Spirit of the Lord is upon me,
  because he has anointed me
  to bring good news to the poor.
He has sent me to proclaim freedom to the captives
  and recovery of sight to the blind,
to let the oppressed go free,
  to proclaim the year of the Lord's favour.
(Luke 4:18–19)

The Old Testament passages that Jesus quotes are from Isaiah 61 and Isaiah 58, which point to a time of future hope. 'The year of the Lord's favour', which comes from Isaiah 61:2, is spoken of frequently in Leviticus 25 as the 'Year of Jubilee'. In Jewish thought, the Jubilee came to be associated with a time of coming deliverance. And so, in claiming to fulfil these scriptures, Jesus is transforming a prophecy about God's future deliverance of his people into a present reality and announcing that his ministry heralds a new era of Jubilee.

The good news Jesus proclaims is all-encompassing, involving liberation that is physical and spiritual, political and economic, individual and national. It extends to all spheres of life and not only to the state of our souls.

In its public ministry, the Church witnesses to this new way of life that is to be found in Christ. It is a radical message of hope and liberation that challenges the dominant narratives of our world today. Over recent years, both the Me Too movement and Black Lives Matter have raised awareness of significant and tragic areas of inequality and prejudice in our society. That such inequality can also be found within the Church is especially troubling. However, the recognition that the gospel is public truth and its claim that 'There is no longer Jew or Greek, there is no longer slave or free, there is no longer male and female; for all of you are one in Christ Jesus' (Galatians 3:28) means that the missional church needs to live this out in its life together. Nineteenth-century Dutch theologian, Abraham Kuyper, who also served as prime minister, passionately believed in the public nature of the truth of the gospel and famously said:

> Oh, no single piece of our mental world is to be hermetically sealed off from the rest, and there is not a square inch in the whole domain of our human existences over which Christ, who is sovereign over all, does not cry 'Mine'!'[8]

Recognising that the gospel is public truth means that the missional church needs to take seriously its vocation to be courageous in calling out all that continues to oppress and hold people captive in our world. It is to speak out against the injustice of racism and prejudice – whether in the world around us or on our doorstep. The church's vocation is to proclaim the life-giving and provocative words that all can be redeemed and made new in Christ. The good news of Jesus Christ has the power to break through the darkness, offering hope and new life to all who would receive.

In a post-Christendom context, the Church needs to move from thinking of itself in ways that look inward and instead realign itself as God's Church for the world. As Newbigin says, 'Churches have been seduced into thinking of themselves as the church of the nation, rather than as the church for the nation, the church that can speak a word of God to the nation.'[9] The greatest gift the Church can offer to the world is to be a new social order, to embody a new way of being community together which challenges the powers and principalities in the world.

The UN Refugee Agency stated that at the end of 2022, there were 108.4 million people who had been forcibly displaced from their place of living, mainly as a result of violence, persecution or violation of human rights.[10] As war continues to ravage many parts of our world, this crisis does not appear to be abating. In the face of such vast global challenges, the Church, even on a local level, has great opportunity to demonstrate what it means to be a new way of being community to those on the margins and to those who are displaced.

Over recent years, Greyfriars Church in Reading has developed a substantial ministry, driven by compassion, dignity and welcome, to those seeking sanctuary in the UK. What started as one remarkable woman's desire to act and provide a house for a family seeking sanctuary has now developed into a whole-church commitment to provide a place of sanctuary for those seeking refuge. In the aftermath of Covid-19, the church set up a drop-in café. Members could 'pay it forward' and leave a donation of a drink or meal behind the counter for those who needed it. The café partnered with the local Refugee Support Trust and other local churches, and once a week local NHS and other services came in to enable people to find support. Many of those who were temporarily housed in a local hostel commented on how unfamiliar and poor the food was, so a conversational kitchen was started, where sanctuary seekers could come to learn English while also cooking food to share with others. Through this ministry, several people have become Christians, been baptised and have integrated into the church family. Others have simply been ministered to and helped by a church that takes seriously the public nature of the gospel, and a new social order that declares all are welcome and can belong.

2 The gospel as story

The second feature we are going to explore is the way in which we are called to share and live the gospel as a story. We noted earlier how Newbigin suggests it is the role of the Church to embody the story of the gospel. He goes on to say this:

The revelation of which we speak in the Christian tradition is more than communication of information; it is the giving of an invitation. It is more than the unfolding of the purpose, which was otherwise hidden in the mind of God but is now made known to us through God's revealing acts; it is also a summons, a call, an invitation.[11]

Telling the story of the gospel to the world is not simply passing on information, like a government information broadcast that issues the latest set of rules and guidance. Instead, telling the story of the gospel is an invitation into a new way of being and seeing the world.

The Massey Lectures is a highly regarded series of public lectures in Canada, featuring some of the world's brightest and best academics and writers – including Martin Luther King, Margaret Atwood and Noam Chomsky. In 2003, the Canadian–American author Thomas King was invited as the first Massey lecturer of indigenous descent to give the series of five lectures. These were published in a book entitled *The Truth about Stories*, with King's central idea being that the stories we tell ourselves and one another shape the world around us.[12] We are a story people, if you like. King commented that 'Stories are wondrous things. And they are dangerous.'[13] The gospel is both a wondrous and dangerous story: wondrous because it narrates the incredible love of God in Christ – the lengths and breadths that God has gone to in the person of Christ to make his love known and present to a broken world. But it is also a dangerous story that threatens the other stories that govern our lives and rule our world. It challenges racial prejudice and pride, consumerism and individualism. It bids us die in order to find new life in Christ. It has the power to turn our lives – and indeed our world – upside down. The gospel is truly the most wondrous and dangerous story there is.

I am part of a group that regularly helps with Sunday services in a local prison. In a place full of people who have been declared guilty in the eyes of the law, there are few who need convincing of the reality of sin. But grace? That's another thing. To stand in the chapel and speak of God's forgiveness, restoration and grace is prophetic evangelism. Seeing some of the men slowly come to see that their life isn't over; that there is a new way; that God loves them and has a plan and a new way for them is one of the most precious pictures of the gospel I have witnessed.

I prayed for Stan during one of his first weeks in prison. He was utterly shell-shocked and terrified. He hadn't for a minute thought he'd end up in prison, and yet here he was. I think he came to chapel to try and find some peace. He shared with me that the wing he was on was very violent and he felt afraid. I prayed for him to experience God's peace and that something would change, and he would feel safe. After I finished praying, he opened his eyes and said, 'Wow, that felt really odd, like pins and needles, but I feel peaceful.' The next week he rushed to tell me that, later that afternoon, he had been moved to a different wing that was much more peaceful and had started to read his Bible and pray, seeking more of the peace he had found in the chapel. His relatively short time behind bars was a journey of accepting what he had done and its consequences, but also a period of discovering a God who loved him and wanted him to live life as part of God's great story of redemption.

One of the most remarkable story-tellers of the previous era was C. S. Lewis, who captured the imaginations of a generation with his fantasy world of Narnia in *The Lion, the Witch and the Wardrobe*. Through the fur coats buried deep within the wardrobe lay a magical world held captive to the oppressive rule of the white witch. The world was awaiting the arrival of Aslan the lion, through whom freedom would come at the cost of sacrifice and resurrection. C. S. Lewis believed that stories could communicate abstract truths of the Christian gospel in a way that felt real and concrete. He believed tales could get past the 'watchful dragons' of religiosity and bring genuine faith:

I thought I saw how stories of this kind could steal past a certain inhibition which had paralysed much of my own religion in childhood. Why did one find it so hard to feel as one was told one ought to feel about God or the sufferings of Christ? I thought the chief reason was that one was told one ought to. An obligation to feel can freeze feelings. And reverence itself did harm. The whole subject was associated with lowered voices; almost as if it were something medical. But supposing that by casting all these things into an imaginary world, stripping them of their stained-glass and Sunday school associations, one could make them for the first time appear in their real potency? Could one not thus steal past those watchful dragons? I thought one could.[14]

For a long time, we have tended to think about sharing the gospel with people in terms of conveying information about Jesus, or verbally convincing people of the truth of the Bible. However, Lewis reminds us of the invitational and storied aspect of our verbal witness. Evangelism as story-telling has been a prominent model of witness in overseas ministry, but in the West our models have been more reliant upon rational apologetics and persuasive arguments. I have a friend who has worked for years as a missionary in the Middle East, and the simple and imaginative task of story-telling has been powerfully effective in introducing people to the Christian faith. Scholar Brian Stone puts it like this in his exploration of evangelism in a post-Christendom culture: 'To become a Christian is to join a story and to allow that story to begin to narrate our lives.'[15]

It might take some shifting in our mindset to think about faith-sharing through story-telling, but in a world fascinated by stories, it is an experiment worth trying. There is certainly a lot of potential here for the artists and creatives in our communities to lead the way.

In addition, we all have our own experience to share of how living within the Christian story has shaped our lives. This doesn't have to be a grand or dramatic testimony (although it may be), but an honest and authentic account of how God's grace and goodness is woven into our everyday lives. It might look like speaking to our friends about answers to prayer we experience, being honest about the struggles we face and talking about the sense of peace which Christ brings in the midst of troubles. Churches can enable this approach by creating a culture of story-telling through Sunday services, home groups and midweek meetings. Hearing one another's stories of hope builds faith and helps those less familiar with this approach think they may be capable of trying something similar.

3 The gospel as discovery

The third idea we are going to unpack is the way in which our own personal discovery of the gospel is something which impacts the way we live and share our faith with others. Being a Christian means that we believe and trust in the gospel. Jesus' call to his first disciples was to 'repent, and believe the good news' (Mark 1:15). Our discipleship journey begins with believing the gospel, and our task as missionary disciples is to witness to the gospel of Jesus. While we know and understand the gospel, it is not a finite thing that can be sealed and packaged neatly. We are on a journey of constant discovery to understand the gospel more fully: the Church hasn't yet grasped all that the gospel means.

This perspective challenges one of the biggest assumptions we make when we think about sharing our faith. We tend to assume evangelism is a one-way street and that the onus is on church, as the possessor of the truth, to do all the talking. We can think that we have a message to bring to the world and all we need to do is deliver it. However, when we recognise that the gospel is of infinite depth and value, we realise that we also are on a journey of discovery. Newbigin expresses this conviction well:

This means that we are engaged in a two-way exercise. We have a story to tell, a name to communicate. There are no substitutes for this story and this name. We have to name the name and tell the story. But we do not yet know all that it means to say that Jesus is Lord. We will have to learn as we go along, as Peter had to learn from his encounter in the household of Cornelius. We are missionaries, but we are also learners, only beginners. We do not have all the truth, but we know the way along which truth is to be sought and found. We have to call all people to come this way with us, for we shall not know the full glory of Jesus until the day when every tongue shall confess him.[16]

I like the way Newbigin reminds us that we are learners as well as messengers. Of course, we have the amazing truth of Jesus to share with people – but we still have things to learn ourselves, and there will always be more to discover about Jesus. The top of the mountain appeared to be a long way away. Looming high above us, its peak piercing the crystal-clear sky, it looked perfect. I knew the views from the top would be stunning, but the question was, how were we going to get up there? The path zigzagged back and forth, steadily climbing thousands of feet, bit by bit. Then, out of the corner of my eye, I spotted what looked like blue cubes suspended in space, and they seemed to be moving: hurrah, a cable car! That decided it. Some of us would walk and some of us would be transported.

The ride up in the cable car was simple but exhilarating. All we had to do was show our pass. Then the gate opened before us and we stepped into a perfect little glass cubicle, which leapt forward and began a steady incline up the mountain. We could see the pathway hundreds of feet below and travellers and climbers steadily ascending, stopping for water and to catch their breath. In a matter of minutes, we, however, were at the top, stepping out into stunning sunshine, breathing in the fresh, unpolluted air and feeling a little light-headed from the sudden change in altitude.

In time, the remainder of the party made it to the top, red-faced and breathless but similarly exhilarated by a route that had been rich in sightings of wildlife and birds. Initially they had followed the wrong fork in the path and had to double back on themselves, but eventually, tired but happy, they also reached the summit. At the top, we all shared the stunning view of the valley below us, as the sun beat down on our faces and birds of prey circled above in a majestic dance routine which seemed like a welcome to this soundless place of wonder.

When it comes to witnessing, many of us hope that sharing our faith with our friends is going to be like the cable car ride. We long for them to get to the view at the top, the beautiful place where the air is clear, and we hope it will be as simple as giving out an invitation and them getting on board. For some people, their journey to faith is indeed like this: God simply intervenes in a miraculous and undeniable way and their life is changed by that one significant encounter. However, for most people, the reality is that in our secular culture, the journey to faith is more circuitous and complicated and can take a significant length of time. And, in any case, we can often find that those who have a dramatic or miraculous moment of healing or encounter have encountered people or milestones along the way that have prepared them for that moment. For most Christians, witnessing to their friends is like accompanying them on a journey up a zigzag mountain path, with twists and turns. We can be sure, however, that the end destination – new life in Christ – is well worth keeping in view.

This idea of fellow pilgrims on a journey is one that has stayed with me as I've sought to find helpful ways of talking about what happens when we share our faith with someone. As mentioned earlier, evangelism can too easily be seen as a one-way street with all the knowledge (and therefore all the power) residing with the Christian. But the reality is that evangelism is an invitation into the story of the gospel, and even if we have been Christians for forty years, there is so much more we still have to discover and experience. I have certainly found in my interactions with people along the pathway to faith that they have taught me things, asked questions I would never have come up with, stretched and challenged me, and made me think in new and fresh ways.

Recognising that the gospel is about what we are discovering too means that witness is always done from a place of humility and openness. When I talk to Christians about what holds them back from sharing their faith with others, the most common answer is fear of coming across as narrow-minded or bigoted. Such fears are not without substance, as the 2022 'Talking Jesus' report demonstrates.[17] Of 4,000 people who were questioned, those who identified as non-Christian gave the following words as most commonly describing the Church: 'hypocritical' and 'narrow-minded' (although, thankfully, 'caring' and 'friendly' followed soon after). It is also distressingly true that people have been seriously harmed by the Church. One only has to read the report coming out of the Independent Inquiry into Child Sexual Abuse in the Church of England and Wales which was published in October 2020 to see the way in which people have been abused by those who had responsibility to care and show compassion.[18] There is no moral high ground from which the Church can sit in judgement on others. Our witness can only begin from a place of personal indebtedness to grace, and a willingness to listen.

Remembering that the gospel is also there to be discovered afresh by us means that we recognise we are receivers of the gift of grace before we are givers. It is interesting that the Apostle Peter, when encouraging the early disciples to 'be ready to make your defence' for the hope that they have, couples this instruction with 'do it with gentleness and reverence' (1 Peter 3:16). Peter knew that the posture of the evangelist was as important as the words spoken, if not more so. We're all aware that it is possible to win the argument but lose the person. Authentic faith-sharing always involves a willingness to accept our own faults as well as a respect for other people's perspectives.

In reflecting on the Malawian practice of hospitality, Kwiyani notes that this is not so much about doing good for another as seeing and welcoming the whole person.

> Malawians believe that when you are hospitable to a stranger you are saying to him, 'You are just as human as I am.' Therefore, in recognising the stranger's humanity, your host is humanized too. A person's hospitality reflects his or her own humanity. To deprive the stranger of his or her humanity – by not being hospitable, for instance – is for the host to deprive him of his humanity too … The guest must also understand that he or she must also be hospitable to the stranger that is his or her host. Hospitality, then, becomes a constant negotiation between two strangers playing host and guest to each other simultaneously.[19]

As I was out shopping one day, I noticed a homeless person sitting on the roadside asking for money. There was a Greggs nearby and, in an effort to offer some kind of help, I thought I would buy this stranger a sandwich. I chose an 'All day breakfast' which looked pretty nice to me and offered it to the man when I came back out onto the street. He looked at me with gratitude in his eyes but said he couldn't eat it because he was vegetarian. I was shocked when I realised. I hadn't even considered that might be the case. I hadn't asked what he would like or afforded him any agency in the decision. I was busy doing what I considered to be a good, Christian, missional thing, but I hadn't really attended to him. Well, that day one of my kids got a nice surprise in their school packed lunch, and I learned a powerful lesson in the importance of listening that helped me recognise where I personally needed to grow in the discovery of the gospel.

To sum up then, the Church is all about the gospel and cannot conceive of itself without this good news. This gospel is both public truth and a profoundly personal story in which we are on a constant journey of discovery.

Four principles for practice

As we seek to live out and proclaim the truth of the gospel, let's consider four principles for practice.

1 Start with what you've got

When we think about the Church's 'strategy' (and we will come back to that awkward word later) for evangelism, we may assume that it starts with a budget, some slick publicity, funding for events and a dynamic and charismatic preacher. However, we actually need to begin with what we have, with what's already 'in our hands' – and that is us. Quite simply, we need to begin with the people we have within our church community, whether that's ten or two hundred. When Jesus commissioned his disciples to go into the world and make disciples, he didn't issue them with a spreadsheet full of targets and KPIs and hand them a wodge of cash. No, he simply appointed and anointed a group of ordinary people, including some who still doubted (Matthew 28:17). We don't have to have life all sorted, and we certainly don't have to be free of questions and doubts, to be appointed and commissioned. God isn't looking for perfection, but he is looking for those who are willing.

So, before we consider events, publicity or courses, we need to think about empowering our churches to see themselves as everyday witnesses to the gospel. Here are a few simple ways your church could to this.

- Teach people the gospel.[20] It's so easy to assume that everyone in church on a Sunday knows what it is to be a disciple. If people aren't excited about Jesus themselves, they're unlikely to share the gospel with others.
- Normalise stories of how people come to faith. Take time on Sunday or midweek to hear how different members of your church found Christ. It can be such an encouragement.
- Find creative ways to pray for people. It could be through prayer triplets or even by choosing a time in the week when everyone pauses to pray – you could set up some kind of timer alert to remind people!
- Gather people according to their place of work and let them discuss what witness might look like as an NHS worker, an office worker, a stay-at-home parent, etc. Invite them to pool their ideas and share these with the rest of the church.
- Identify the capital 'E' evangelists and encourage them to mentor someone else in the church.
- Audit how much time people are spending on 'in-house' church activities. For example, if you find yourself too busy to have time with non-church friends, perhaps consider what you might give up.

We won't become an effective community of missionary disciples overnight. And rather than suddenly implementing a new mission action plan or strategy, it might be more effective to start small and gradually turn things up.

My kids love to listen to loud music, and sometimes when I come into the kitchen to do something, it is way too noisy for me. I have learned that if I just turn the volume down to a respectable level, they will notice and I will inevitably be met with cries of, 'Why did you do that? I was listening to that!' However, if I just gently move the volume down one notch and then a few minutes later another notch, we eventually end up with something much more pleasant!

Perhaps the reverse could be true in our churches. If we suddenly crank up the evangelism volume overnight, people might find it too much; it might jar uncomfortably with our current approach. However, if we gradually raise the temperature bit by bit over a period of time, we can slowly and purposefully become more missional and intentional in our ministries.

My friend moved to a church which hosted a thriving parent and toddler group. However, although the group met in the church hall and was free, it seemed completely unrelated to the church. To have suddenly introduced a strong Christian element would have jarred and potentially felt manipulative to those who had made this their community. So, over time, my friend just gradually raised the temperature. Initially this took the form of a brief but friendly welcome: 'Hi, we're from the church and we're delighted to host this community gathering. We're here if you need anything.' This led to conversations and friendships being formed. My friend was then able to introduce a fun Christian song that the toddlers and their carers could join in with if they liked. Eventually this led to more interest and at Christmas, she was able to invite people to stay on after the original playgroup for a short 'Messy Christmas' celebration to which many came. Now friendships have developed to the point where she is hoping to invite the parents and carers to Bible study or Alpha. Being intentional and prayerful is bearing fruit.

Here are a few ways you could turn up the evangelistic temperature in your church.

- Start praying intentionally for people in your local community, particularly those who connect with your church's activities. Pray for them by name!
- Work on your welcome. Ask a friend (either from another church or a non-church friend if they would be willing) to attend your church as a 'mystery worshipper' and give you feedback on how welcoming you are. What might you need to change in the light of their feedback? Do people say hello to newcomers or just talk to their friends? Does the noticeboard

need an overhaul? Is the coffee lukewarm and served in ancient mugs? Invest in developing a great welcome.

- Use the Christian festivals creatively. Produce invitations for people to invite friends and consider having a community barbecue or meal after major services. An All Souls' service, offering a quiet and peaceful space to reflect and light a candle, could draw in those who have lost a loved one recently. Or offer a fresh 'take' on a traditional service – one city church I know created goody bags for a local hostel as part of an urban Harvest Sunday celebration.

- Create brief but punchy content for social media. A two-minute testimony can work well and does not require much IT skill. A vicar recently told me that he had seen more people come to his church through TikTok in the last six months than by any other means. Be creative and bold!

- Focus on children and young people – they are, after all, the missing generation from the Church. My friend Andy holds a 'Blessing of the book bags' service every September. He invites the children from the local schools to bring their book bags into church that Sunday and prays with them for the new year. A village church in Hampshire held a Christmas challenge and hid dozens of stones painted like baby Jesus around the village. People had to post their location on social media with the hashtag #JesusRocks!

- Ask what might need to stop in order to create space for something new. Tom moved to a church which had been running Messy Church on a Saturday for several years. However, no families from outside the church ever came, and it was using a lot of resources and energy. Making the radical decision to stop created some unhappiness, but as time has passed, the space, resources and energy for something new has opened up and it is engaging with unchurched families. That might never have happened if the status quo had remained.

- Audit your community. What are the issues people care about in your local area and how can the church make a positive contribution? It might be as a simple as clearing up litter or carol singing in a local residential home. Are there people in your churches who have skills to share with the local community, like teaching cooking or mending electrical appliances?

- Write down all the activities the church undertakes, from Sunday services and midweek home groups to foodbanks and drop-in cafés, and ask the question, 'What one thing could we do to increase the opportunities for sharing the gospel?'

In a sense none of this is rocket science, nor is it some radically new strategy to change the world. However, the steady, prayerful and courageous work of being intentional about reaching out in new and creative ways is at the heart of missional church.

2 Pursue creativity

It was a in a rare moment of silence at family teatime that my youngest son proudly announced, 'Today was a good day, I learned to God-bridge.' As an evangelism lecturer, I was curious to hear of this new and unfamiliar apologetic approach, and my ears instantly pricked up. Listening further, I discovered that God-bridging is in fact a technique in the computer game Minecraft which involves placing building blocks at a certain angle as your character is running.

However, the phrase 'God-bridging' got me thinking about the way we approach the gospel as story. The reality in our secular context is that the concepts and ideas it contains have less and less resonance for the society around us. Sin, salvation, redemption and sanctification are not topics at the top of people's discussion lists. This lack of interest in Christian theology must not be mistaken for a lack of interest in the spiritual per se, however. The fact that over seventy million people have downloaded the meditation app Headspace onto their phones is indicative of a desire for wholeness and peace. We're all interested in ultimate meaning and purpose, in discerning what is of value, in knowing how to have inner peace and future hope. The issue is that many people do not think the Church will be able to help with any of those quests. Our task as a witnessing community, therefore, is to create bridges between people's experiences and relevant concepts of the gospel story, so that they might be able to hear and receive the invitation of new life.

In 1998, the new Choluteca Bridge in Honduras was commissioned for use. At over 400 metres long, it was considered an engineering masterpiece. The bridge's strength was soon to be tested though, as later that year, Honduras was tragically hit by Hurricane Mitch. Although many other bridges and roads were damaged, the Choluteca Bridge stood firm, relatively unscathed by the raging storms around it. However, despite the brilliant Japanese engineering, the Choluteca Bridge was useless. The hurricane may not have impacted its structure, but the roads leading to the bridge on both sides had been washed away by the extensive rainfall, and the Choluteca River, over which the bridge had been built, had carved a new course. Due to the extensive flooding, it was now flowing off to the side. The Choluteca Bridge stood intact over dry land and rapidly won the nickname 'the bridge to nowhere'.

It is an apposite analogy for some of our cherished evangelistic models and practices which no longer make the connections we need them to. As a student in the 1990s, I remember being asked a lot about how I could trust the Bible was true. I memorised all the stats and facts about numbers of manuscripts so I could effectively answer people's questions. I haven't been asked about the veracity of the Bible in over twenty years! That isn't to say it's not an important question, but it's not one people are actually asking. We would do well to listen and observe, so we can become better at connecting the gospel story with issues that really do seem to matter to people.

Of course, Paul in Athens is a master of this approach. In Acts 17, he carefully takes in those aspects cherished in the culture around him and uses them as his starting point as he shares the Christian story. For us, engaging with books, films and music can be a great way of bridging the gap and making connections between issues people are thinking about and the deeper themes of the gospel.

In July 2023, Barbenheimer was all the rage as two blockbuster films were released simultaneously. People found themselves debating whether to see the *Barbie* movie or *Oppenheimer* first, with many opting for a double bill and watching them consecutively. In a sense, the films couldn't be more different, with Greta Gerwig's *Barbie* advertising a candy-pink, fluffy delirium in contrast to the hard-hitting, sombre feel of Christopher Nolan's *Oppenheimer*. However, both films, in very different ways, attended to one of the most crucial questions at the heart of the Christian gospel: what does it mean to be human? *Barbie*, it turned out, was not the fluff some people anticipated but actually dealt humorously and articulately with the question of authenticity, the importance of the role of the Creator in a quest for personal identity, and even the significance of death and mortality. *Oppenheimer's* exploration of the creation of nuclear weapons during the Second World War dealt profoundly with humanity's capacity for the creation of evil and terror and even its justification. Films such as these, and others like them, serve as a snapshot of a cultural moment of which the Church should not remain ignorant. Watching, critiquing and – dare I say it – enjoying such cultural phenomena with friends and family outside the Church is a way of building bridges, leading not only to greater relationships but also to conversations that take us into a deeper engagement with values, meaning and purpose.

We need a new generation of engineers to design bridges between church talk and everyday talk where the gospel is unfamiliar and its significance unrealised. We can start with something as simple as a trip to the cinema with a friend, or a discussion in the doctor's surgery waiting room about the latest Netflix series. In our churches, we can create spaces which prepare us for those conversations, weaving into sermons and Bible studies some kind of engagement with these cultural moments, so the whole church is better equipped for moments when they arise.

3 Create spaces for people to explore faith

Our third principle demonstrates the importance of creating safe spaces where people can explore faith in an unpressurised and supportive way. With the media seeming to delight in telling us about the rapid decline of the Church, it is understandable that we are preoccupied with numbers. As I mentioned briefly in the introduction, the most recent UK Census, published in 2022, indicated a fall from 59.3% (in 2011) to 46.2% (in 2021) of people identifying as Christian.[21] A 2021 report by the Church Commissioners suggested that over 350 church buildings might close by 2026 – a rate that seems likely to be accelerated by a post-Covid church attendance drop of one third.[22] However, we also hear stories of new churches being planted and of churches who are seeing significant growth among the younger, so-called 'missing generation'. One of these is Saint Church in Hackney, which has become a thriving community of worshippers, many under the age of thirty. While fully aware of the statistics of decline, Al Gordon, the entrepreneurial leader of the Saint network of churches, said in a recent interview:

The average age of a churchgoer is increasing, and there are less of them. And that is one story. But the other story we're seeing is people who pray, who have a spiritual hunger, that curve is going the other way.[23]

If there is indeed increased spiritual hunger, how then might we create spaces for people to explore faith in a safe and accessible way?

My friend Alice was a regular school gates chatterer – you know, one of those mums who's actually positive and full of energy first thing in the morning. Over the years, as she dropped her two children at the local school, she had got to know some of the parents and carers in the local area. Chatting in her easy and natural way, she discovered a number of children were coming home from the church-led assemblies full of questions about life and Jesus and the Bible. Many of the parents said they didn't know how to answer these and, in fact, found they had questions of their own.

So, Alice took the plunge and invited a group of mums to her house the following Friday. Over a simple lunch of soup and cheese, she created a space for people to ask questions about faith and to explore the Bible together. It became evident that there was real spiritual hunger and the group gathered momentum, always finishing in time to pick up the kids from school. Now between fifteen and twenty mums meet each Friday lunchtime in multiple homes (they outgrew Alice's kitchen table!).

One of them, Beth, had attended church on a Sunday her whole life, but it was only when she learned to pray with others that a sense of personal call was awoken. Another, Tamara, had recently escaped an abusive relationship and was very protective of her young son. Life had been so full of battling and struggle that initially she wouldn't allow others to get close to her. However, something kept her coming to this group and eventually it became a safe place where she could learn to trust others. In time, she came to learn to trust Christ too and her life was turned upside down by grace.

Creating spaces, whether that is through established courses such as Alpha, Christianity Explored, Pilgrim, or in a more home-grown way as outlined here, is crucial for the missionary church. What step might God be calling you to take to create such a space?

4 Develop a strategy for discipleship

There we have it – the 's' word. Sometimes we can feel uneasy talking about a strategy for making disciples, but the reality is that, if we aren't intentional, then it won't happen. While Jesus didn't dole out a ten-step handbook to his close followers on how to make disciples, he did nevertheless give a clear indication that making disciples wouldn't happen while they were sitting in their PJs watching Netflix. Rather, he required them to go, to teach and to baptise people who would follow him wholeheartedly.

I recently watched a video about Apple's marketing strategy and was intrigued by how it makes you feel you belong. You are invited in, never pressurised. The staff are more than happy to allow you to linger as you try out gadgets (I usually find it very hard to get my kids to leave the Apple store). In fact, you are invited to touch, to experiment, to imagine how this thing might fit with your lifestyle, to imagine how it might make your life better. Apple staff never speak badly about other equivalent products, but simply and winsomely demonstrate what a difference theirs will make to you – and all the focus is most definitely on you.

There are not many in our culture today who are actively seeking Jesus or who have questions about the Bible, but there are many looking for meaning and purpose, and asking how and where they can find happiness and fulfilment. The huge increase in the wellbeing industry bears this out. We know the one who said, 'I came that they may have life, and have it abundantly' (John 10:10). We know that he has so much more to offer than a gadget which might make your life more effective, streamlined or even entertaining. We know the one who can truly make us whole and offer life in abundance. Going to church is one of the ways in which people can taste and see and experience something of that life. But for many there are barriers to attending and changing that won't happen overnight.

We need to take seriously the task of discipleship because none of us is a blank piece of paper, simply waiting to have the gospel story written on us. Rather, we are complex tapestries of stories, experiences and ideas that have shaped us, some in good ways and some in negative, harmful ways. Unpicking those threads is a costly task and one we need to be prepared to accompany people through as we introduce them to the one who takes our brokenness and weaves it into something beautiful. We need to acknowledge that in our post-Christian world there is no quick fix discipleship; there's no six-week course that will sort out everything. We have to be prepared to invest time, build community and journey with people.

Max grew up in an ordinary family in East Sussex, but his dad left when he was six and he didn't get on well with his stepdad. Max struggled to fit in at school and always felt he was the odd one out. He started to lark around and get in trouble to get himself noticed and win some friends, smoking and drinking to numb the pain. In his teenage years, he drank more and began experimenting with drugs. However, he still felt as if he didn't really belong or fit in, and deep down he believed that he wasn't really good enough or worth much.

As his drinking and drug use escalated, Max began stealing to feed his habit and getting into trouble with the police. He never lasted long in a job as he was unreliable, often going to the pub at lunchtime and failing to return. Max described his life as 'chaotic'. Things came to a head when his partner got pregnant and gave him an ultimatum – it was either her or the drugs. Desperate to keep her, he stopped the drugs, but the drinking got more and more intense. One day, he went to the pub with some friends and they all drank hard. When his friends eventually left, Max felt too ashamed to go home to his partner, so he stayed there drinking his sixteenth pint of the evening, all alone.

A rather ordinary looking guy came over to him, sat down at the table and asked, 'Are you OK? You seem kind of lost.' Max admitted that he was. The guy stayed and chatted with him and said that he wanted Max to know that God loved him no matter what. He told Max he should think about going to the church next door.

That night Max went home and in a drunken state said to his partner, 'I'm going to start going to church.' His partner was not religious at all and laughed this off, assuming it was the alcohol speaking. The next morning, she said to him, 'You said the funniest thing last night.' 'I know,' Max said, 'I'm going to start going to church.' So that Christmas they went to a children's carol service with their young daughter, and Max found he couldn't stop crying throughout the service. He felt overwhelmed by feelings of warmth and homecoming. But he couldn't make sense of this and brushed it off. He wanted desperately to change but thought he'd have one last binge that Christmas. Unfortunately, this binge involved drinking 1.5 litres of gin, smashing up his car and his partner walking out on him.

That next week, Max returned to church and began attending a drug and alcohol recovery programme. Over the next few weeks and months, he discovered that what the stranger had said to him in the pub was true – God was real and God loved him no matter what. His partner came back now he had stopped drinking, and together they did an Alpha course, and both said yes to Jesus. They joined a home group and began to embed themselves into the life of their local church community, making friends who helped them in their new life in Christ. When I met Max, he had just been baptised along with their daughter and new baby in the sea (which he said was definitely colder and more pebbly than he expected). Max is now free from addiction and fully immersed in the life of the church, living a life he never imagined would be possible.

If our churches are to be places where individuals like Max and others can find their way into new life in Christ, then we must take discipleship through community seriously. We need to heed the call to build friendship and create space for people to belong and to be loved. In our post-Christian world, the church is not just an add-on once someone has made the journey to faith. It can be the very place where faith is introduced and nurtured, sometimes over a significant period of time. As communication specialist Pierre Babin expresses it:

> The aim of evangelization becomes the Christian community, and its main medium is also the Christian community. Recognition of this is essential in defining our pastoral options: the medium is the community of believers themselves. It is their dynamic faith, their lifestyle, and the witness they bear to having been healed and saved by Christ.[24]

The church community itself is not only the vessel of the message of the gospel but the means through which the gospel is proclaimed, embodied and ultimately encountered.

Discussion

1 Reflect on the idea of the gospel as public truth. What are some of the issues today that you think the gospel challenges and addresses in our society? How should the Church respond?

2 Think of a TV show, film or book you have recently enjoyed. How might that be a starting point for talking about the good news of Jesus?

3 Review all the activities your church does to connect with people outside the church. How could you turn up the temperature one notch on each of them?

6
Church as dependent: The role of the Spirit in mission

It was my thirty-second birthday and I was enjoying a meal with a small group of friends in a local Thai restaurant. The remnants of wrapping paper and envelopes lay strewn on the table as we were served our food. It was only a small place, but all the tables were full, and a buzz of chatter and laughter filled the air. Suddenly the lights were dimmed and the waitress came out the kitchen holding a large chocolate cake adorned with candles and sparklers. The whole restaurant joined in the singing of 'Happy Birthday' as the cake was proudly placed in front of me. I looked in surprise at my friends, struggling to believe that they had gone to all this effort for a thirty-second birthday!

Nevertheless, I smiled and enthusiastically blew out the candles on the cake. That was when I noticed carefully iced writing that read, 'Happy Birthday Nicky'. A sudden realisation dawned upon me. I was not in fact the intended recipient of this cake. Standing up, I sheepishly asked, 'Is there someone here called Nicky?' A few tables away, a woman with a somewhat disappointed look on her face, sitting opposite a red-faced man, raised her hand. There was nothing for us to do but rouse the restaurant in another (by this time slightly less enthusiastic) rendition of 'Happy Birthday', with a loud 'NICKY' as the cake was deposited in front of the right person.

This final chapter is all about the gift of the Holy Spirit and the first question we must ask is: who is the intended recipient of this gift? The Old Testament Scriptures frequently point to the extraordinary and dramatic work of the Spirit of God through particular individuals, enabling them to do miraculous and often unexpected things. For example, Gideon was a somewhat nervous and ordinary individual until the Spirit of God came upon him and through him brought deliverance to the entire nation (Judges 6:34). In the case of Ezekiel, the Spirit came upon him and transported him to a valley of dry bones (Ezekiel 37:1). The Spirit is also active in using people as bringers of his message. Pharoah recognises that Joseph is 'one in whom is the spirit of God' since he could interpret Pharaoh's terrifying dreams (Genesis 41:38). The prophets of old saw themselves as those through whom the Spirit of the Lord was speaking. Micah declares, 'I am filled with power, with the spirit of the LORD, and with justice and might' (Micah 3:8). While the anointing of the Spirit in the Old Testament was upon particular people, anointed for a special task, the prophet Joel prophesied about a time when the Spirit would fall more generously and fully upon all, regardless of age or status.

> I will pour out my spirit on all flesh,
> your sons and your daughters shall prophesy,
> your old men shall dream dreams,
> and your young men shall see visions.
> (Joel 2:28)

Waiting for the Spirit

In the book of Acts, the risen Jesus is quite clear that the disciples are to wait for something. Before he ascends to heaven, he tells his them to go back to Jerusalem and await a special gift (Acts 1:4). Despite their questions, Jesus is not to be drawn on precise timings, saying, 'But you will receive power when the Holy Spirit has come on you; and you will be my witnesses in Jerusalem, in all Judea and Samaria, and to the ends of the earth' (1:8). Perhaps some of the disciples didn't mind huddling away and waiting. With Jesus now physically gone from their presence, they may have felt scared at the prospect of being identified as his followers and staying indoors would be a welcome relief. For others, this might have been frustrating after the euphoria of seeing Jesus come back to life and witnessing him walking through walls. They were ready to spring into action, but Jesus had told them to wait. What were they waiting for? Didn't they have what they needed to get on with the job?

We can experience this kind of tension in the Church today too. Faced with a narrative of church decline and increasing antagonism and apathy towards the Christian message, it can be tempting to hide away and wait until things calm down. Maybe a better season is just around the corner, so we should just focus on keeping our house in order, preserving what we have, and maybe venture out of church again when we're feeling strong enough. Some of us, though, may be facing the temptation to rush into action immediately. Driven by a panic mentality, we grab whatever last chance there might be to grow the Church, presuming that doing something is at least better than doing nothing.

But Jesus told his disciples to wait – for the gift of the Spirit.

This command rebukes our tendency to assume that 'good results' are dependent upon our strategy and skill, and even our enthusiasm. Missionary theologian John Taylor describes the Holy Spirit as the 'Chief Actor' in the mission of the Church, and even suggests that for Jesus himself, his identity and mission were 'derived from his self-immersion in that flood tide of the Spirit'.[1]

Throughout the book of Acts, a consistent link is made between the mission and the Church and the gift of the Spirit. That the Spirit is a gift given particularly and especially for the Church in mission is evident by the nature of this manifestation at Pentecost. Not only do the gathered disciples experience the rushing wind and tongues of fire, but their experience of the Spirit propels them out of their hiding place to the gathered community outside, where they speak the good news of Jesus in familiar and unfamiliar languages. This moment of Spirit-empowerment has significant consequences, and Luke tells us that some three thousand people become followers of Jesus that day (Acts 2:41). The intended recipients of the gift are initially the apostles, but as they see the Joel prophecy fulfilled before their eyes, it becomes clear that the nations are also intended recipients of the special gift.

It is the prophecy in Joel that Peter refers to on the day of Pentecost, as he seeks to make sense of the extraordinary events unfolding. Public preaching in multiple languages was not a consequence of a night of drinking, as some people joked – rather, it was the outpouring of the Spirit of God, not on a select few, but on all people. Taylor puts it like this: 'What they had seen in Jesus and now experienced in themselves was the same dynamic and creative *ruach*, now available in that unprecedented way that the prophets had foretold.'[2]

The Spirit continues through the book of Acts to come upon the apostles in ways not unlike those seen in the Old Testament: for example, Philip, like Ezekiel, finds himself transported to a different place after his encounter with the Ethiopian official on the road to Gaza (Acts 8:39). The disciples perform miracles (Acts 3:6–8) and are filled with strength to speak to rulers and authorities with an uncharacteristic boldness (Acts 4:8). However, the message is clear that the Spirit is not just for certain or special people but for all disciples of Jesus. Luke declares that, 'All of them were filled with the Holy Spirit' (Acts 2:4) and that a new era had dawned. The same Spirit that was upon Jesus as he pronounced good news for the oppressed and the poor was now filling all those who believed in the risen Jesus and was empowering them for the task of witness. Just as there can be no talking of being a disciple of Jesus without also being a witness to Jesus – since they are one and the same thing – neither can there be any talk of the Holy Spirit in the life of the disciple without a concern for mission and witness. The Holy Spirit is given to the Church for the task of witness.

The beginning or the end?

On 28 July 2022, the soap opera *Neighbours* screened its final and 8,903rd episode. Former stars such as Jason Donovan and Kylie Minogue reprised their roles as Scott and Charlene to bid a final farewell to the one of the most cherished fictional residences, Ramsay Street. I have to confess to feelings of nostalgia as I remembered a TV show I had loved; its start time of 5.35 p.m. remained emblazoned on my mind two decades after I had stopped watching. But the end was nigh, and after thirty-seven years, the adventures of Ramsay Street reached a final crescendo with 2.5 million viewers tuning in in the UK – the highest numbers of viewers since 2008. However, only a few months later, the cast and crew of *Neighbours* were delighted to announce that a new broadcasting service had been found and the show was being recorded once more. The adventures of Ramsay Street are not over yet and continue with new twists and turns.

At the end of the book of Acts, Luke makes clear that while one chapter might be closing, this is no finale. His recording of Paul's journey might have come to an end, as we see Paul finally make it to Rome, the economic and political capital of the ancient world. However, the mission of the Church was only just beginning. Luke records Paul talking about the Holy Spirit speaking through the prophet Isaiah and closing with these words: 'Let it be known to you then that this salvation of God has been sent to the Gentiles; they will listen' (Acts 28:28). Paul might have made it to Rome, but the work of the Holy Spirit was not yet done. In fact, it had only just begun.

Roland Allen served as a missionary for many years in North China, where he worked with the Society for the Propagation of the Gospel. In 1927, he published a book called *Missionary Methods: St Paul's or ours?* which was both a penetrating critique of the Western missionary movement of the nineteenth century, and also remarkably forward thinking in identifying some of the issues that post-colonialism would later raise.[3] One of the central reflections was to ask how self-supporting the churches in places such as China and Africa really were, and whether Western missionaries had failed to trust that the Spirit, who was at work at Pentecost, was still alive and working today. Allen sought to ask the Western Church what could be learned from Paul's model of mission as a pattern for our own engagement with cultures different from our own – not least Paul's dependence upon the Holy Spirit as the one who sustains and enables the ongoing growth and work of the Church:

> We have imagined ourselves to be, and we have acted so as to become indispensable. In everything we have taught our converts to turn to us, to accept our guidance. We have asked nothing from them but obedience. We have educated our converts to put us in the place of Christ. We believe that it is the Holy Spirit of Christ which inspires and guides us; we cannot believe that the same Spirit will inspire and guide them.[4]

Allen challenged a tendency within many of us active within mission to assume that ultimately success, or even flourishing, depends upon us. He lamented the lack of trust in the supreme and all-encompassing work of the Spirit, the sort that enabled Paul to leave Thessalonica in a hurry but still trust that God was at work.

Amos Yong is a contemporary scholar, seeking to demonstrate the centrality of the Spirit to our thinking about mission in the Church's present experience. His book *Mission After Pentecost* presents a breathtaking overview of the work of the Spirit from Genesis through to Revelation.[5] It demonstrates that the work of the Spirit in mission is not limited to the events of Pentecost only, but that the ministry of the Spirit at Pentecost is the culmination of all that the Spirit has already been doing through the Old Testament. In this way, Yong suggests that it is not simply that we need a *missio Dei* but we need a *missio Spiritus* to direct us: in other words, missional church today cannot hope to move forward without rooting itself firmly in the Spirit of mission. Without the Holy Spirit, the Church is left waiting in the upper room. The Spirit is the engine of the missional church.

The Holy Spirit and the mission of the Church

Since Jesus' life and ministry was entirely dependent upon the work of the Spirit and the first apostles were also reliant upon the infilling of the Spirit, so we too need the empowering gift of the Spirit. In his final conversations with his disciples, Jesus makes clear that he will send another like himself to continue to guide them (John 16:13). Taylor emphasises the connectedness between Christ and the Holy Spirit in the life of the disciples:

> By taking permanent hold of the waiting disciples as he had taken hold of Jesus, the Holy Spirit effected a kind of extension of the incarnation, bringing them into everything that could be available to them in Christ. This was their 'christening' by which they were made to be as Christ in the world, his body filled with his very Spirit.[6]

Taylor's understanding of the Spirit and mission is not so much that the Spirit equips disciples for particular special tasks but that the presence of the Spirit of Christ enables disciples to embody Christ in the world. For Taylor, this is the mission of the church, and it is inextricably linked to the presence of the Spirit.

> The mission of the church, therefore, is to live the ordinary life of men in that extraordinary awareness of the other and self-sacrifice for the other which the Spirit gives. Christian activity will be very largely the same as the world's activity – earning a living, bringing up a family, making friends, having fun, celebrating occasions … and so on. Christians will try to do all these things to the glory of God, which is to say that they will try to perceive what God is up to in each of these manifold activities and will seek to do it with him by bearing responsibility for the selves of other men.[7]

In the midst of this call to be filled by the Spirit and positioned outwards, the task of evangelism is a natural and necessary responsibility in order to make others aware of who Christ is. But for Taylor, this is not the task of a gifted individual; rather it is an ecclesial matter as churches form and point towards the generous invitation of God in Christ:

The church is essentially scattered, like seed in the earth, salt in the stew, yeast in the dough. The Christian's milieu is the world because that is the milieu of the Holy Spirit. Yet the units of the scattered church are not Christian individuals, but twos and threes gathered together to provide the 'one-another-ness' in which the Holy Spirit possesses them ... We must expect the 'little congregations' to take different forms and fulfil different functions precisely because they are meant to match the circles and circumstances in which human life and need presents itself.[8]

There are two important lessons here. First, this connectedness between the Spirit of mission and the life of the disciples means that we cannot contemplate the idea of Church apart from mission. Mission simply cannot be an optional extra for the Church; nor can it be only for particular kinds of churches or special people who might engage in certain mission activities. The Spirit's ministry is both ecclesial and missional, both church-shaped and mission-shaped. This requires a shift in our mindset from imagining mission as something the Church does or as, in some way, one of the many options available to it. Mission is integral to what it is to be a community indwelt by the Spirit.

Second, this focus also realigns us, prompting us to recognise that all our missional endeavours are dependent upon the Spirit of God. Newbigin understands the early church's missional engagement to stem from their Spirit-filled lives. He suggests that our tendency to talk about mission and evangelism in terms of duty and obligation does not tally with the way the first disciples understood their calling. A vibrant, Spirit-filled spirituality means mission is inevitable and natural rather than a matter for begrudging obedience:

It is, is it not, a striking fact that in all his letters to the churches Paul never urges on them the duty of evangelism. He can rebuke, remind, exhort his leaders to faithfulness in Christ in many matters. But he is never found exhorting them to be active in evangelism ... Mission in other words is gospel and not law; it is the overflow of a great gift, not the carrying of a great burden.[9]

This means that there is no place for pessimism when we think about the work of mission in the world today, despite what church attendance statistics might look like. Ultimately, it is a work of the Spirit. Both our best and worst efforts are entirely dependent upon God's gracious breathing of his Spirit afresh into our lives and our world. Strategy is important but ultimately, it cannot save us, only God can. William Abraham expresses this well:

> What is needed is not just more talk, or more programmes of church growth and evangelism, but the mysterious power of the Holy Spirit present in both our hearts and blowing afresh in our worship, in our proclamation, and in our deeds.[10]

Spirituality, therefore, proceeds strategy. What we desperately need in the church today is not a new or better strategy but a renewed spirituality. At the end of the day, mission is a matter of the heart rather than a matter of finance and numbers.

Spirit-shaped mission

Let's now explore three ways in which a theology of the Spirit might shape the way we think about the missional task.

1 The Holy Spirit is at the heart of human relationality

Yong makes this point in reflecting on the opening words of Genesis, where the Spirit of God was hovering above the waters at the beginning of creation (Genesis 1:2). He adds that not only is the Holy Spirit transcendent above creation, he is also immanent within it, since all living creatures are constituted by God's 'breath of life' (Genesis 1:30). Furthermore, we read in the subsequent chapter that humanity (Adam and Eve) is brought to life through God's own breath (Genesis 2:7). The Hebrew word that conveys breath, *ruach*, is often used to describe the Spirit of God in the Old Testament. In Greek, the corresponding word is *pneuma*, which gives us pneumatology, which essentially means a theology or study of the Holy Spirit. Yong draws a connection with the book of Acts and, in particular, Paul's statement in Athens in which he notes that their poets write, 'in him we live and move and have our being' (Acts 17:28). Yong suggests that all humans have this shared breath of God in common with one another, since it is integral to our very humanity.

John Taylor describes the Holy Spirit as the 'go-between' God and emphasises how our openness to God is connected to our openness to those around us.

> The Holy Spirit is the power which opens eyes that are closed, hearts that are unaware and minds that shrink from too much reality. If one is open towards God, one is also open to the beauty of the world, the truth of ideas, and the pain of disappointment and deformity. If one is closed up against being hurt, or blind towards one's fellow-men, one is inevitably shut off from God also. One cannot choose to be open in one direction and closed in another. Vision and vulnerability go together. Insensitivity also is an all-rounder. If for one reason or another we refuse really to see another person, we become incapable of sensing the presence of God.[11]

This emphasis on the horizontal as well as the vertical dimensions of the Spirit's ministry can be a helpful starting point in mission, preventing us from too easily slipping into an 'us and them' mentality, where we tend to focus on our differences rather than our shared humanity. The recognition that all of human life begins with the breath of God gives us confidence that, while we seek to impart the good news of Jesus, there are connection points with the world around us. It enables us to focus on our shared humanity in our relationship with others, rather than our difference, which is a powerful apologetic in a society that tends towards increasing polarity and division.

2 The Holy Spirit is transnational and transcultural

The Old Testament is full of missiologically-directed promises of what the Holy Spirit will one day do. For example, Joel foretells a time when all people will receive the Spirit in a different, powerful and dynamic way. In Ezekiel, we see how Spirit-filled foreigners are now incorporated into the people of God. In the famous passage of the dry bones (Ezekiel 37), the Spirit is poured out upon Israel in a way that is visibly observable to a watching world. Yong writes:

> Surely here there is no direct or casual interface between the outpouring of the divine *ruah* and the repentance and salvation of the nations, but there is no overlooking the fact that the salvation of Israel will occur in terrestrial, even cosmic, daylight, observable by the world. The explicit missiological point to be underscored is that the work of the divine *ruah*, while focused on the internal dimensions of Israel's life before God, has transnational implications and reverberations.[12]

This sense of the Spirit being poured out in such a way that the world watches and takes note is of course magnified in the book of Acts, where it is precisely the Spirit who constantly prompts the newly Spirit-filled disciples on an outward trajectory. The book of Acts makes spectacularly clear that it is the Holy Spirit who brings to fulfilment the Old Testament promises that God's people would be given a new Spirit and that this Spirit would go out to the ends of the earth. Yong suggests that the list of nations in Acts 2:5–11 is a shortened list of the Old Testament 'table of nations' in Genesis 10, and so what is happening at Pentecost really is the 'ends of the earth' receiving the gospel. Throughout the book of Acts, that impetus of the 'ends of the earth' is driven by the ministry of the Spirit, prompting Peter to visit Cornelius and blowing through the physical storms of Paul's missionary journeys until he ends up at

Rome itself. From the very outset, the Spirit of God is intent on crossing boundaries of race, culture and class and weaving the nations of the world together into a rich tapestry. This means that in our thinking about mission, there always has to be consideration of those who are not like us, those who are excluded, on the margins or beyond our current scope. The Spirit of God is the boundary-crossing breath of God.

3 The Holy Spirit is concerned with the whole of human life

One final aspect of Spirit-shaped mission that we are going to explore is the idea that the Spirit is engaged in the concerns and cares of daily human experience. It is often the case that discussion about the Spirit in the Church can tend towards the abstract and the experiential. However, the outpouring of the Spirit on Pentecost impacts the whole of human life. Okesson helpfully points out that what the Spirit does, through the translation of the gospel into multiple languages, is to draw both Jew and Gentile believers into a 'new thicker whole, where "all the believers were together and had everything in common" (Acts 2:44), reorientating the ways they undertook economics, family and social activities (Acts 2:45–7)'.[13] The Spirit in Acts is not only manifest in verbal witness but also in justice. Yong points out the connection between the disciples being filled with the Spirit and their sharing of the common life. He cites Barnabas as the exemplary disciple who sells his land and lays the profit at the apostles' feet (Acts 4:36–7). In the same way that Jesus' declaration in Luke 4 (often called the Nazareth Manifesto) made clear the social and economic impact of the good news of the gospel, so throughout the book of Acts, the ministry of the Spirit is seen both in the preaching of the gospel and also in social and economic ways, such as the daily distribution of food (Acts 6:1) and in Paul's speaking truth to power and insisting that powers act justly (Acts 16:35–40). Yong writes:

> Just as the gift of the Spirit had socioeconomic consequences in instantiating, even if preliminary, the year of Jubilee

aspirations of the poor and oppressed, so also does this manifestation of the divine breath have public and political implications for worldly kingdoms.[14]

The book of Acts ends with a strong sense that the Spirit who was at work in conversion and social justice through the first disciples is still at work today. For Christians today, this gives us confidence to look for signs of the Spirit at work in the world around us and to understand our discipleship not only in terms of private devotion but public words and action. Many churches have begun to take creation care as a serious contribution to their missional approach, which is entirely appropriate when thinking about the missional Spirit. There is work to be done. The *missio Spiritus* is still on the move.

Four principles for practice

Let's now consider four principles for practice of a *missio Spiritus* for the Church today:

1 Be imaginative

On 22 February 2011, an earthquake struck the city of Christchurch in New Zealand. Measuring 6.3 on the Richter scale, the quake was catastrophic, claiming the lives of over 180 people and injuring thousands. Over 50% of the city's buildings were damaged which impacted the economy significantly, not least as they were due to be hosting the rugby world cup later that year. One iconic building that was irreparably ravaged was Christchurch Cathedral. Its spire collapsed and the entire building became structurally unsafe. In the months and years that followed, the cathedral was at the centre of a heated debate about its future: demolish the remaining structure and start again, or try and preserve the historical building? While legal battles ensued and the decision to repair the damaged building was not made until a decade later, an interim solution for the worshipping life of the city was found. Japanese architect Shigeru Ban designed a stunning transitional cathedral made of reinforced cardboard tubes, laminated wood and triangular stained-glass windows. Ban never intended his famous cardboard cathedral to be permanent, and it stands as an icon of innovation and environmental sustainability in a city that has rebuilt itself after tragedy and trauma.

Though I have sadly never seen this cathedral in situ, it appeals to me as a symbol of missional innovation in a time of upheaval. The tendency (particularly for Anglicans like me) is to think of the Church as a fixed institution, with our responsibility during times of cultural earthquake to preserve and maintain what we already have. Perhaps the transitional cathedral is an architectural example of Newbigin's notion of the Church as the pilgrim people of God, chastening our desire for permanence and stability and instead encouraging us to pursue adventure and movement. In his poem, 'Choruses to the Rock', T. S. Eliot expressed this notion of the Church constantly building, constantly decaying and being attacked from outside rather starkly.[15]

A missional spirituality has innovation in its DNA. In the Old Testament, it is the Spirit of God that is frequently connected with the new thing God will do – for example, in Ezekiel when God speaks of the new covenant, it is a 'new spirit' that will usher in this change. It is the Spirit who shakes up the established ways of doing things – for example, in the Joel 2 prophecy, it is through the ministry of the Spirit that previous distinctions of age, gender and social status are eradicated.

In August 2015, *Songs of Praise* broadcast a special episode from a church which had been built in a weekend. St Michael's was made out of corrugated iron and tarpaulin and sat in the middle of what was known as 'the jungle' – the Calais camp for migrants, many of whom had risked everything in search of safety and asylum. The church provided a temporary sanctuary for many Ethiopian and Eritrean Orthodox believers, who were able to find solace and God's peace in the hellish circumstances around them. In the words of priest and journalist Giles Fraser who visited the church: 'Forget those fancy churches that end up being museums for the 1% – this is a holy place'.[16]

In 2016, St Michael's was bulldozed to the ground as part of the move to close down the camp. While the church is no longer there, for a brief moment of time it provided spiritual sustenance and life to many at the very lowest point in life: it was a beacon of hope in the midst of despair, a visceral example of temporary church. And where people in need find connection with a God who sustains them in their darkest hour, even if just for a season, is this not holy ground? Though written in the 1960s, Catholic theologian Hans Kung's words on the temporality of the Church still speak resonantly: 'Essentially an interim Church, a Church in transition, and therefore not a church of fear but of expectation and hope; a Church which is directed towards the consummation of the world by God.'[17]

In a slightly different context, Sanctuary Marquee is a pop-up church at the annual Glastonbury Festival, providing spiritual solace and opportunity for exploring the Christian faith through a variety of services, including baptisms and marriage blessings. One girl told how she went to Glastonbury and soon realised her friends were only interested in taking drugs. She instantly felt isolated. The pop-up church was a safe space, where she found friendship and a home for her 'homeless soul'.[18]

There are plenty of other examples of pop-up church, just for a season: a prayer tent at a local festival, opportunities to pray for healing for Saturday morning shoppers on the high street. One church in east London put up a huge Christmas tree and invited local residents to write prayers to God which they enclosed in see-through baubles and prayerfully hung on the branches. While it is important with such pop-up endeavours to consider how people might be connected longer-term with more permanent expressions of church, part of our response to the *missio Spiritus* is to seek those places where the light needs to shine and to be willing, even if just for a season, to bring hope. Imagination is one of the gifts of the *missio Spiritus* to the church today.

2 Tradition and innovation go together

It is hopefully not hard to see how imagination and innovation are gifts from the Spirit to the missional church. Indeed, we can sometimes view the Spirit as the maverick member of the Trinity, off doing his own thing! However, innovation and tradition are not polar opposites competing for our attention, and it would be a mistake to assume tradition has no part to play, for the Spirit is always and forever bringing us back to Christ. Paul declares in 1 Corinthians 12:3, 'no one can say, "Jesus is Lord" except by the Holy Spirit', while Jesus makes clear to Nicodemus in their night-time conversation that 'no one can enter the kingdom of God without being born of water and Spirit' (John 3:5). The Spirit is forever bringing people to new life in Christ. However, the Spirit is also the one who brings us into connection with one another. As 1 Corinthians 12:12–13 states:

> For just as the body is one and has many members, and all the members of the body, though many, are one body, so it is with Christ. For in the one Spirit we were all baptised into one body – Jews or Greeks, slaves or free – and we were all made to drink of one Spirit.

In as much as the Spirit leads us imaginatively into new things, the Spirit is also the one who draws us to Christ and roots us in the faith once proclaimed by the apostles. It is this message of new life in Christ which never changes or goes out of fashion. Paul Barnett comments on what it was that made the early church grow with such rapid momentum:

> The birth of Christianity and the birth of Christology are inseparable. New Testament churches grew out of Christological preaching and were characterised by Christological worship. Attempts to define the birth of the church by sociological or psychological grounds are doomed to failure – Christological conviction was the engine that drove early Christianity.[19]

Paul Barnett argues that it was this simple and passionate focus on Jesus which was the key to the growth and momentum of the early Christian movement. In the Holy Spirit, there is both the propulsion to look outwards in creative and new ways and also the pull to be anchored in Christ, the source of life. The Great Commission itself is a call to both innovation (making disciples of all nations) and anchoring (baptism, teaching and obedience). Innovation and tradition work as partners with one another – encouraging us to be creative and courageous in finding new ways to share the gospel, while also keeping us rooted in Christ and Scripture.[20]

I love *The Great British Bake Off*. Each season, it's great to see the fresh faces in the Bake Off tent, eager to demonstrate their skill and creativity, each imagining that one day they might receive the holy grail of baking – the Hollywood Handshake. I especially like the biscuit challenge, where gingerbread creations struggle to triumph over gravity and the sweltering heat of the tent, often subsiding at the crucial moment, to the frazzled baker's dismay. But my favourite weekly challenge is the showstopper.

The showstopper relies upon innovation and creativity. Bakes are rewarded for their originality, imagination and sometimes their sheer ambition. However, the bakers that excel tend to be those whose knowledge of the rudimentary tasks of baking is strongest. You can have all the creativity in the world when planning your cake, but if the basic ratio of eggs, flour and butter is not precise, the whole project is doomed from the start. The greatest chefs and bakers in our world today are often those who have spent considerable time learning the ropes as a sous chef – that foundation gives them the freedom to bring something beautiful and incredible to life.

In 2020, a Spanish journalist interviewed the Pope on the impact the pandemic was having upon the Roman Catholic Church. Pope Francis spoke of our tendency to think of the Church as a fixed institution that has no flexibility or ability to adapt, and our presumption that creativity is to be found in abandoning the rigid and restrictive institutionalisation of the Church. He commented:

It is the Holy Spirit who institutionalizes the church, in an alternative, complementary way, because the Holy Spirit provokes disorder through the charisms, but then out of that creates harmony. A church that is free is not an anarchic church, because freedom is God's gift. An institutional church means a church institutionalised by the Holy Spirit. A tension between disorder and harmony: this is the church that must come out of the crisis. We have to learn to live in a church that exists in the tension between harmony and disorder provoked by the Holy Spirit.[21]

Pope Francis challenges the dichotomy that is sometimes too readily imagined between new (or fresh) expressions of church and tradition. The Holy Spirit is the one who institutionalises the Church – in other words, the one who establishes and makes it real – and is integral to the unity and stability of the Church, as Paul writes in Ephesians 4:3–4: 'making every effort to maintain the unity of the Spirit in the bond of peace. There is one body and one Spirit, just as you were called to the one hope of your calling'.

The Spirit both anchors us to Christ and connects us to one another, but also calls us out and beyond to new and imaginative expressions. It is the work of the missional Spirit to enable the Church to proclaim afresh the gospel story in word and deed and liturgy in each generation. However, in our pursuit of the novel and the fresh, we would do well not to ignore the treasures at our feet. Cherishing the liturgical worship that has been handed down from generation to generation might prove to be our salvation in an era of constant change and the pursuit of the new and the temporary. Theologian Andrew Walker expresses this connection between the new and the old like this:

> Praying the prayers of the church is to pray not with second-class material despoiled by time, but handed-on treasures that resist and overcome the corrosions of time.[22]

While many young adults are inevitably drawn to new and more relevant expressions of church, there will also be those who appreciate the anchoring that a more traditional or contemplative expression of worship can provide. For a generation brought up on fast food, quickly changing video game entertainment, and often a lack of stability both at home and in the political world around them, there is a hunger for permanence and a sense of rootedness. Tradition might not be the enemy of innovation that we sometimes assume it is. Contemplative services can also provide a sense of connectedness, not only with history (praying prayers handed down the generations), but with people across the world, and the recognition that we are a global community – like an antidote to a polarised society. Among a generation attuned to wellbeing and positive mental health, the silence and stillness of reflective worship can be an inviting oasis in a world of noise and distraction. As American scholar and pastor Leonard Sweet puts it: 'Postmodern pilgrims must strive to keep the past and the present in perpetual conversation so every generation will find an expression of the gospel that is anchored solidly to the faith that was once delivered.'[23]

3 Step outside your comfort zone

In a quote attributed to André Gide, French author and winner of the Nobel Prize for Literature, 'Man cannot discover new oceans unless he has the courage to lose sight of the shore.' The *missio Spiritus* does not reside in the static and the comfortable, but is on a constant journey to accompany the gospel to the ends of the earth. For the first apostles, the infilling of the Spirit was a huge dose of courage – a great encouragement, in that very moment, to leave behind the safety of their holy huddle and to become early morning preachers on the streets. The transformation in Peter alone is remarkable – from one who was so afraid he denied Jesus three times, to one who stands before a crowd of thousands and declares, 'Therefore let the entire house of Israel know with certainty that God has made him both Lord and Messiah, this Jesus whom you crucified' (Acts 2:36). Peter is no longer timid and afraid, but courageous and bold. The difference is the Spirit.

The Spirit's work in this regard is two-fold. First, the Spirit equips disciples with boldness to step outside of their comfort zone (towards the ocean!), and to speak confidently of their faith with renewed courage. Jesus promised his disciples that this would be one of the things that the Spirit would do among them:

> When they bring you before the synagogues, the rulers, and the authorities, do not worry about how you are to defend yourselves or what you are to say; for the Holy Spirit will teach you at that very hour what you ought to say.
> (Luke 12:11–12)

When my friend Tom became a Christian, he was wary of what he considered to be the dubious practice of evangelism. One day, a few weeks after he had encountered God in a powerful way, he said emphatically, 'I am not going to be one of those Christians that's into evangelism'. However, as our conversation progressed, Tom opened up about how his newfound faith in Christ prompted him to begin to restore some of the broken relationships in his life. He followed this up with, 'The funny thing is, since I have started following Jesus everyone has been asking me about it and I have had loads of interesting conversations with people about my faith.'

While this story demonstrates the dissonance that so often exists between people's negative preconceptions about evangelism as something weird and unnatural and the actual experience of simply sharing our story of faith, it also shows the work of the Spirit in believers to overflow in natural ways such that they simply can't help but talk of the things of God. At the other extreme, there are of course incredible stories of Christians throughout the world who are persecuted for speaking out about their faith. It is often evident that the supernatural empowering of the Spirit has enabled great courage under such pressure and oppression.

However, the second way in which the Spirit moves us from the shore to the ocean is by prompting us to look in unexpected places for signs of God's presence and grace. For Peter, his journey from comfort zone to missional adventure didn't end at Pentecost. When he visited Cornelius, he crossed barriers of culture, race and social expectation. And he was surprised to find that God had got there before him! God was already at work in a surprising and unexpected way and God's Spirit had gone ahead, forever committed to the task of the making disciples to the ends of the earth. It is significant that, for both Peter and Cornelius, this encounter originated in prayer. In Acts 10, Peter is on his roof at noon praying when he falls into a trance and sees the bizarre vision of unclean animals. He hears God telling him that three visitors are arriving and that he must go with them. As we have heard, he is taken to the Gentile centurion Cornelius' house and entering – an act that would have been considered unthinkable for a Jewish man – discovers that four days previously Cornelius had also received a vision from God. This course of events and the revelation of the Spirit to both Peter and the Gentile stranger before him causes Peter to announce, 'I truly understand that God shows no partiality, but in every nation anyone who fears him and does what is right is acceptable to him' (Acts 10:34–5).

It is important not to underestimate the significance of what is happening here. For Peter to declare there is no partiality and that Cornelius is an equal recipient of the grace of God is revolutionary – it is an epoch-defining moment in the life of the Church. And it is the work of the Spirit who has led Peter here, prompting him both physically through miraculous signs and also moving his heart from prejudice to recognition that God's grace is broader and wider and deeper than he had hitherto imagined. In this moment, Peter sees that the Christ who gave him a second chance is the God of second chances for all who would cry out to him. As if to underline that this miraculous coming together of Jew and Gentile is a work of the Spirit, the Spirit falls upon them all and collectively they praise and worship God.

And so, in this wonderful story, Peter discovers that the Spirit goes ahead of him, preparing the ground, stirring the hearts of those he is calling to himself, and all Peter has to do is follow and seek the signs of God's Spirit already at work. It is only by the work of the Spirit that Peter has courage to leave behind the familiarity of the shoreline and step out into the oceans of God's grace, poured out in unimaginable and miraculous ways. Alan Roxburgh describes this Spirit-inspired missional task thus:

The Spirit is out there, ahead of us, inviting us to listen to the creation groaning in our neighbourhoods. Only in the willingness to risk this entering, dwelling, eating and listening will we stand a chance as the church to bring the embodied Jesus to the world.[24]

My friend Paul is the pastor of a community church in Oxfordshire. The church recently moved into a new building which is located on a housing estate that's still in the process of being built. In November, the developers put up a Christmas tree and proposed a date for the switching on of the lights. Paul was quick to reach out to ask the developer whether the church could be involved, and perhaps sing some Christmas carols before the big switch on. The developer was more than happy for the church to be present and on the night, over seventy showed up as carols were sung and some Christmas Bible passages were read. This was the beginning of new relationships being formed, purely through the taking of a small step outside the comfortable and familiar. The following day, the developer commented to Paul that in all his years of working in housing development, he had never experienced anything quite like this before.

Turning up and singing carols didn't require vast resources and skill, but it did require the prompting of the Spirit and a bit of courage. Where might the Spirit be prompting you to get outside your comfort zone and see where God is already at work? Who knows what God might do?

4 Prayer is the starting point/the secret place

Through this chapter, we have been slowly building the case for one of the most fundamental convictions of the missional church: dependency on the Spirit of God. There can be a tendency in new and shiny mission initiatives to elevate pragmatics above spirituality, with our methodology leading our theology rather than vice versa. However, the *missio Spiritus* calls us to recognise that all the energy and direction for mission and its ultimate effectiveness stems not from our own efforts and creativity, but from God.

Yong points to Paul's image of the 'jars of clay' in 2 Corinthians as an apt metaphor for mission in a post-Christendom world:

> But we have this treasure in clay jars, so that it may be made clear that this extraordinary power belongs to God and does not come from us. We are afflicted in every way, but not crushed; perplexed, but not driven to despair; persecuted, but not forsaken; struck down, but not destroyed; always carrying in the body the death of Jesus, so that the life of Jesus may also be made visible in our bodies.
> (2 Corinthians 4:7–10)

Participating in the *missio Dei* means we are empowered by the Spirit, but that does not mean the missional task will be easy or constantly successful. The presence of Christ within us is often made visible through weakness, and our hope is that the extraordinary God works through our ordinary efforts. Yong describes this Spirit-led approach to mission as:

> one that depends not on the machinery of a centralized missionary operation but on the power of the Spirit to work in and through the mundaneness of creaturely agents. This is the apologetics born not from eloquence but from the finitude and perishability of 'clay jars' (4:7) albeit infused with the Spirit.[25]

Missiology that is dependent upon pneumatology starts and ends with prayer. Prayer is the discipline of a missional spirituality. Prayer is the engine of any strategy for mission. After the initial hubbub of Pentecost preaching, the first task of the early church was prayer: 'They devoted themselves to the apostles' teaching and fellowship, to the breaking of bread and the prayers' (Acts 2:42).

The devotion to prayer was not individualistic but done in community, as the early church gave themselves also to the apostles' teaching and the breaking of bread. This pattern of consistent and corporate prayer happens again and again throughout the book of Acts. When Peter and John have their first run-in with the authorities, the church gathers together in prayer (4:2). When James is killed and Peter imprisoned, the church prays fervently for his release (12:5). When Paul and Barnabas appoint elders to lead the fledgling church plant in Antioch, they teach the church to pray (14:23). Paul begins nearly all his letters with the assurance that he is praying for those to whom he is writing: 'We always give thanks to God for all of you and mention you in our prayers' (1 Thessalonians 1:2).

Such devotion to prayer is more than a transactional exercise or habit, by which we present our requests to a divine slot machine in the sky, hoping for a good outcome. For Taylor, missional prayer introduces us both to a deeper awareness of others with whom and for whom we pray, while also bringing us into greater communion with God. Hence his description of the Holy Spirit as the 'go-between' God. This dependence upon our communion with Christ is essential for the missional church.[26]

In a culture which preaches self-reliance and empowerment, humble dependence upon God in prayer is a radical choice. Though Taylor wrote in the 1970s, his challenge to find the 'nerve to pray' and develop the discipline of joyful and expectant prayer has never been more relevant than in our own particularly secular moment:

> We have to challenge the reported death of God, even while we feel in ourselves the evidences of it. We have to defy the habits of thought that tell us prayer is meaningless, remembering that other ages also found it so. But we also need the endurance to learn a long-lost art and recover functions that have started to atrophy.[27]

It remains a fact of the history of Christian mission that periods of most intensity and revival seem to be always accompanied by a renewal of prayer. The Celtic missionary saints Columba and Aiden were devoted to prayer and founded communities of prayer wherever they travelled. On 13 August 1727, the newly formed Moravian community, which met at Count Zinzendorf's estate in Germany, experienced a Pentecost-like event which led to a renewed zeal for prayer, which led to a 24/7 prayer vigil which lasted over one hundred years! This community impacted a generation of missionary individuals including John Wesley who sought, by the grace of God, to revive the established Church through the preaching of personal repentance and forgiveness, and who was himself fiercely disciplined in personal prayer. The thriving churches in the Global South today are accompanied by a vibrant and prayerful spirituality of joyful dependence upon God. For the missionary church, prayer can never fall out of fashion.

In chapter 2, I wrote about the walls of my church, and I have shared something of its journey towards growth and mission. It was in 1997, when we had moved to south London, that I pulled up at Peckham Rye station on the train ride into work and saw this large Victorian church building. I heard the gentle voice of God telling me that this was the church I was meant to be going to. That evening, I mentioned this to my husband to see what he thought, as we were planning to start attending one of the large churches in the city, full of other young adults. He looked at me in surprise. That very day, a friend of his had told him he should go and try All Saints Peckham. We went to our first service the following Sunday and met a diverse congregation of about twenty, meeting in a vast building with paint peeling from the walls and no working central heating, while the adjoining hall had been condemned as unsafe. The service itself was somewhat chaotic: there was one person playing a simple keyboard on chord function, another enthusiastically on accordion, a third on tambourine – and a tangible sense of joy-filled hope. It wasn't like anything I'd been to before, but it already felt like home.

All Saints Peckham had been established in the Victorian era by a returning missionary from India named Revd Thomas Gaster. The church building itself was built in 1867 in response to the new village that was growing in Peckham and was designed to seat around six hundred. The church hall next door housed a thriving children's ministry in the Victorian era. However, as I mentioned earlier, like many other established churches in Britain, All Saints Peckham saw steady decline from the post-war era onwards. While immigration, particularly from the Caribbean, bolstered the church in the 1960s and 70s, it continued to decline to the twenty or so who were present that autumn day in 1997 when we first visited.

Earlier that year, a new part-time vicar by the name of Bob Hurley had been appointed to All Saints Peckham, also taking on a part-time role as diocesan missioner. At his interview, he had been informed about the church development plan the diocese had put in place in response to the vastness of the building and its dwindling congregation. The plan was to knock down the church and church hall, sell the land to private developers and construct a little purpose-built community centre for the twenty church members. Bob was asked at the interview whether he understood the development plan and he said yes, he did understand, but as he wrote later, 'understanding a thing is different to agreeing with it.'[28] He met a handful of the elderly ladies, mainly Black Caribbean, at the interview and asked them only one question: 'Do you believe God can fill this church?' 'Yes,' they replied. 'We just need someone to lead us.' When Bob was offered the job later that day, he knew God was calling him and God was at work in Peckham.

The first challenge Bob had to address, as he and his family moved in, was the church development plan. The diocese had already spent thousands of pounds on architects' fees and things were well under way. However, a new bishop had recently been appointed, and one day Bob was summoned to his office and asked why he was opposing the plans that had already been agreed. Bob replied:

I believe in a God who builds churches, and who causes them to grow, He doesn't knock them down. I believe that He wants to fill All Saints Church, and He wants it to be a light to the community.[29]

Swayed by such conviction and enthusiasm, the diocese agreed to put the development plan on hold and Bob was given two years to grow the church to at least forty-five and install heating to make the building functionable.

Within six months, the congregation had increased to forty-five, and within two years, the church had well over one hundred members and had become the fastest growing Anglican church south of the river. At the proposed meeting with the diocese to discuss the development plan, Bob deliberately left the heating on for twenty-four hours so the church was boiling hot! He thought the diocese would never close a warm church.

An entire book could be written on those two years alone, analysing what factors led to the extraordinary growth in the period. Bob was a passionate preacher, rooted in Scripture, and his sermons were challenging and encouraged personal discipleship. Bob was also an evangelist – people were forever giving their testimony at the front about how they had bumped into Bob and how he had led them to Christ. Small groups were started, enabling discipleship and community. The building was cleaned up, the front gardens cleared, the hall made safe. Funds were provided miraculously to install heating and a sound system, making services more appealing and accessible. Young professionals moved into the area, priced out of more expensive neighbouring Clapham, and got stuck in with leading Sunday school and youth outreach. Mission was the priority, and the desire of the growing leadership of the church to be local, compassionate and evangelistic focused the church's attention outwards. Any one of these factors could have had an influence, and the combination of them all was potent. But the secret of growth lay somewhere else.

What Bob found out as he led this church was that the group of women he had met at his interview knew how to pray. A number of them had joined the church in the 1970s when they had migrated to Britain. Two of these women, Guerline and Nesta, had come from Barbados in their early twenties and, despite not being made to feel welcome by some of the existing congregation, had decided All Saints would be their spiritual home. One of the first things they had done was to set up a Thursday night prayer gathering where they could pray freely and passionately in a way that was unfamiliar to many in the Church of England. Mavis, a Jamaican powerhouse of intercession and faith, was a spiritual mother to many in this group and beyond, and someone who impacted my own spiritual journey profoundly with her faith-filled obedience and prayer. These three, along with others including Dorene, Icy, Anne, and Nesta's son Peter (who often led them in hymns on the accordion), met every Thursday night for nigh on forty years. If the buses were running then, come rain or shine, they would be there. There was no heating in the church, and yet even in the depths of winter these women would meet, hats, coats, and scarves on as they walked round the little electric heater, praying that God would build his church in Peckham. Nesta and Guerline shared with me a time they had all received the same picture from God of shoots of grass growing up little by little. Through this picture, they believed God was saying that the church would once again be full, especially with children and young people. For twenty years, even as things continued to decline and they were presented with architects' plans for a small chapel to house them, they kept praying for a full church, trusting in Jesus' promise that he would build his Church and that even the gates of hell would not prevail against it (Matthew 16:18).

Bob left in 2002, and we have had three further ministers since then who have built on this foundation, experienced further growth and seen the church through challenges as well as triumphs. Some of our great generation of prayer warriors are now with the Lord they loved and served so faithfully, and their funerals have been some of the most joyful I have ever attended, but the Lord continues to hear the prayers of the faithful. These women serve as a powerful reminder that strategy will only take us so far and that prayerful dependence upon the Spirit remains the way that God will build and grow his Church. To these women, I dedicated this book and I am indebted to them. I pray God raises up another generation like them.

We began this book with Newbigin's central conviction that what the world needs is not a new strategy or rational apologetic but a Church that lives out the gospel message. As we peer into the future, we cannot know what lies around the corner. We don't yet see the new ways the Church might express its common life in loving witness, nor the new opportunities to connect the life-changing gospel of Jesus with the lives of those around us. Equally, we do not know the new challenges that will be levelled against the gospel, or the courage we may need. However, what we do know is that Jesus has promised to build his Church and nothing will stand against it. This is not triumphalist rhetoric but a call to deep trust in the God of mission who has given us his Spirit. My hope and prayer is that this book has encouraged you to think in new ways about being missionary disciples and how together, by God's grace, we might live out his story in the world today.

Discussion

1 How has your understanding of the Spirit been shaped by what you have read? What has been your experience of the Spirit in your own life?
2 Can you think of a time when you have been prompted by the Spirit to step out of your comfort zone? What happened?
3 What do you find easy or hard about prayer? How can we encourage one another in our churches to pray more?

Notes

Acknowledgements

1 Frederick Buechner, *Wishful Thinking: A theological ABC* (London: Bravo Ltd, 1993).

Introduction

1 'Religion, England and Wales: Census 2021', *Office for National Statistics*, 29 November 2022, https://www.ons.gov.uk/peoplepopulationandcommunity/culturalidentity/religion/bulletins/religionenglandandwales/census2021 (accessed 6 January 2024).

2 Cited by Anglican Ink, Kaya Burgess, 'Britain is no longer a Christian country, say frontline clergy', *The Times*, 30 August 2023, https://anglican.ink/2023/08/30/britain-is-no-longer-a-christian-country-say-frontline-clergy/ (accessed 6 January 2024).

3 Harvey C. Kwiyani, *Multicultural Kingdom: Ethnic diversity, mission and the church* (London: SCM Press, 2020).

4 C. S. Lewis, *God in the Dock: Essays on theology and ethics* (Grand Rapids: Wm. B. Eerdmans, 2014 edition), p. 240.

5 Hendrick Kraemer, cited in David J. Bosch, *Transforming Mission: Paradigm shifts in theology of mission* (Maryknoll, New York: Orbis Books, 1991), p. 2.

6 Lesslie Newbigin, *The Gospel in a Pluralist Society* (Grand Rapids, MI: Wm. B. Eerdmans, 1989), p. 227.

7 Lesslie Newbigin, *The Light Has Come: Expositions on the fourth Gospel* (Handsel Press Ltd, 1982), p. 228.

8 John G. Stackhouse Jr (ed.), *Evangelical Ecclesiology: Reality or Illusion?* (Grand Rapids, MI: Baker Academic, 2003), p. 9.

9 Lesslie Newbigin, *The Household of God* (London: Paternoster Press, 1998).

10 Newbigin, *The Household of God*, p. 22.

11 Trevin Wax, 'Pessimistic About the Future? You need "gospel bearings"', *The Gospel Coalition*, 26 January 2017, https://www. thegospelcoalition.org/blogs/trevin-wax/christians-need-gospel-bearings-when-pessimism-is-all-the-rage/ (accessed 6 January 2024).

Chapter 1 – Church and mission

1 Emil Brunner, *The Word and the World* (London: SCM, 1931), p. 108.
2 For a more detailed analysis of the term 'missional' see my earlier work, *New World, New Church: The theology of the emerging church* (London: SCM Press, 2017).
3 Darrell Guder (ed.), *Missional Church: A vision for the sending of the church in North America* (Grand Rapids, MI: Wm. B. Eerdmans Publishing Company, 1998).
4 Darrell Guder, *Called to Witness: Doing missional theology* (Grand Rapids, MI: Wm. B. Eerdmans, 2015), p. 168.
5 'Canada Mourns as Remains of 215 Children Found at Indigenous School', *BBC News*, 29 May 2021, https://www.bbc.co.uk/news/world-us-canada-57291530 (accessed 6 January 2024).
6 Brian McLaren, *A Generous Orthodoxy: Why I am a missional, evangelical, post/protestant, liberal/conservative, mystical/poetic, Biblical, Charismatic/contemplative … emergent, unfinished Christian.* (Grand Rapids, Michigan: Zondervan, 2006), p. 106.
7 Geoffrey Bromiley and T. F. Torrance (eds), *Karl Barth: Church Dogmatics* (Peabody MA: Hendrickson, 2010), vol IV, part 3.2, p. 568.
8 Guder, *Missional Church*, p. 6.
9 Christopher J. H. Wright, *The Mission of God: Unlocking the Bible's grand narrative* (Oxford: IVP, 2006), pp. 22–3.
10 Walter Brueggemann, *Genesis: Interpretation: A Bible commentary for teaching and preaching Genesis* (John Knox Press, 1982), p. 105.
11 Christopher J. H. Wright, *The Mission of God's People: A Biblical theology of the Church's mission* (Grand Rapids: Zondervan, 2010), p. 72.
12 Christopher J. H. Wright, 'Integral Mission and The Great Commission: The five marks of mission', *Lausanne-Orthodox*

Initiative, https://www.loimission.net/wp-content/uploads/2014/03/
Chris-Wright-IntegralMissionandtheGreatCommission.pdf (accessed
18 December 2023).

13 Guder, *Missional Church*, p. 6.

14 James K. A. Smith, *You Are What You Love: The spiritual power of
habit* (Grand Rapids: Brazos Press, 2016), p. 23.

15 Lesslie Newbigin, *Truth to Tell: The gospel as public truth* (London:
SPCK, 1991), p. 86.

16 Lesslie Newbigin, *Proper Confidence: Faith, doubt and certainty
in Christian discipleship* (Grand Rapids, MI: Wm. B. Eerdmans
Publishing Co, 1995), p. 76.

Chapter 2 – Church on the move

1 Richard Niebuhr, *Christ and Culture* (Harper and Row Publishers,
1956).

2 Callum G. Brown, *The Death of Christian Britain* (London:
Routledge, 2000), p. 193.

3 Steve Bruce, 'The Demise of Christianity in Britain' In G. Davie et al
(eds), *Predicting Religion: Christian, secular and alternative futures*
(Surrey: Ashgate Publishing Limited, 2003), p. 53.

4 Harriet Sherwood, 'Church of England expects attendance to fall for
next 30 years', *The Guardian*, 17 February 2016.

5 Hard Believer, 'First Aid Kit', *YouTube*, 27 August 2009, https://www.
youtube.com/watch?v=DDG8xqz7BIk (accessed 18 December 2023).

6 Stephen Hance, *Seeing Ourselves as Others See Us: Perceptions of the
Church of England* (Grove Books Ltd, 2021).

7 Martyn Percy, *Engaging with Contemporary Culture: Christianity,
theology and the concrete church* (Abingdon: Taylor & Francis Group,
2005), p. 2.

8 James D. Hunter, *Before the Shooting Begins: Searching for democracy
in America's culture war* (The Free Press, 1994), pp. 200–1.

9 Trevor Hart, 'Through the Arts: Seeing, Hearing and Touching the
Truth', in Jeremy Begbie, *Beholding the Glory: Incarnation through the
Arts* (Baker Publishing, 2001), p. 19.

10 Smith, *You Are What You Love*, p. 172.

11 Smith, *You Are What You Love*, p. 173.

12 Smith, *You Are What You Love*, p. 174.
13 Hart in Begbie, *Beholding the Glory*, p. 16.
14 Francis Schaeffer, *Two Contents, Two Realities* (London: Hodder & Stoughton, 1974), p. 17.
15 Timothy Tennent, *Invitation to World Missions: A Trinitarian missiology for the twenty-first century* (Grand Rapids, MI: Kregel Academics, 2010), p. 22.
16 Tennent, *Invitation to World Missions*, p. 23.
17 Lamin Sanneh, *Translating the Message: The missionary impact on culture* (Maryknoll, New York: Orbis Books, 1989), p. 8.
18 Sanneh, *Translating the Message*, p. 60.
19 Darrell, L. Guder, *The Continuing Conversion of the Church* (Grand Rapids MI: Wm. B. Eerdmans Publishing Co., 2000), p. 73.
20 Newbigin, *The Gospel in a Pluralist Society,* p.153–4.
21 Barth, *Church Dogmatics,* vol IV, part 3, p. 720.
22 Graham Cray, 'Communities of the Kingdom' in Graham Cray and Ian Mobsby (eds), *Fresh Expressions of Church and the Kingdom of God* (Canterbury Press, 2012) p. 18.

Chapter 3 – Church as presence

1 David Bosch, *Transforming Mission*, pp. 412–3.
2 Lesslie Newbigin, *The Open Secret: An introduction to the theology of mission*, second edition (Grand Rapids, MI: Eerdmans, 1995), p. 121.
3 Church Commissioners for England, 'From Anecdote to Evidence: Findings from the Church Growth Research Programme 2011–2013', 2014, *Church of England*, https://www.churchofengland.org/sites/default/files/2019-06/from_anecdote_to_evidence_-_the_report.pdf (accessed 18 December 2023).
4 Michael J. Gorman, *Becoming the Gospel: Paul, participation and mission* (Grand Rapids, MI: Wm. B. Eerdmans, 2015), p. 43.
5 Gorman, *Becoming the Gospel*, p. 65.
6 Newbigin, *The Gospel in a Pluralist Society*, p. 227.
7 Henri Nouwen, *Life of the Beloved: Spiritual living in a secular world* (New York: Crossroad Publishing Company, 1992), p. 30.
8 Common Worship: Holy Communion Service, *Church of England*,

https://www.churchofengland.org/prayer-and-worship/worship-texts-and-resources/common-worship/holy-communion-service (accessed 2 January 2024).

9 Sam Wells, *Incarnational Mission: Being with the world* (Norwich: Canterbury Press, 2018).

10 Daniel W. Hardy, *Finding the Church: The dynamic truth of Anglicanism* (London: SCM Press, 2001).

11 Hardy, *Finding the Church*, p. 4.

12 Steve Aisthorpe, *Rewilding the Church* (St Andrews Press: Edinburgh, 2020), p. 195.

13 Cited in Mary Ellen Hines, *Companion to the Calendar: A guide to the saints and mysteries of the Christian calendar* (Chicago, IL: Liturgy Training Publications, 1993), p. 147.

14 Jürgen Moltmann, *The Crucified God: The cross as the foundation and criticism of Christian theology* (Minneapolis: Fortress Press, 1993), p. 22.

15 Mark Gornick and Maria Liu Wong, *Stay In the City: How the Christian faith is flourishing in an urban world* (Grand Rapids, MI: Wm. B. Eerdmans, 2017).

16 Gornick and Wong, *Stay In the City*, p. 15.

17 Charles Dickens, *A Tale of Two Cities* (William Collins Reprint Edition, 2010), p. 5.

18 Richard Bewes, *Wesley Country: A pictoral history based on John Wesley's journal* (Worthing: Creative Publishing, 2003).

19 Samuel Escobar, *The New Global Mission: The gospel from everywhere to everyone* (DG Illinois: IVP Academic, 2003), p. 94.

Chapter 4 – Church as community

1 Alan Jamieson, *A Churchless Faith: Faith journeys beyond the churches* (London: SPCK, 2002).

2 Stanley Hauerwas, *Resident Aliens: Life in the Christian Colony* (Abingdon Press, 1989), p. 58.

3 Rowan Williams in Cray and Mobsby, *Mission-Shaped Church*, p. vii.

4 Paul S. Minear, *Images of the Church in the New Testament* (Presbyterian Publishing Company, 2004).

5 Minear, *Images of the Church in the New Testament*, p. 25.

6 It was while working as the Prime Minister's Chief Spokesperson that Alastair Campbell famously said 'we don't do God' when Tony Blair was asked about his Christian faith.

7 Robert Webber, *Ancient–Future Evangelism: Making your church a faith-forming community* (Grand Rapids: Baker, 2003), p. 78.

8 Webber, *Ancient–Future Evangelism*, p. 78.

9 Colin Gunton, *The Church on Earth: The roots of community* in Colin Gunton and Daniel Hardy (eds), *On Being the Church: Essays on Christian community* (Edinburgh: T&T Clark, 1989); Miroslav Volf, *After Our Likeness: The Church as the image of the Trinity* (Grand Rapids, MI: Wm. B. Eerdmans, 1998).

10 George Eldon Ladd, *A Theology of the New Testament* (Grand Rapids, Michigan: Wm. B. Eerdmans, 1993), p. 284.

11 Ladd, *A Theology of the New Testament*, p. 385.

12 Wayne Meeks, *The First Urban Christians: The social world of the Apostle Paul* (Yale: Yale University Press, 1983).

13 Meeks, *The First Urban Christians*, p. 191.

14 Willie James Jennings, *Acts* (Kentucky: Westminster John Knox Press, 2017), p. 115.

15 Jon Yates, *Fractured: How we learn to live together* (London: Harper Collins, 2022), p. 21.

16 'UK: Six million UK adults don't know any of their neighbours by name', *Aviva plc*, 30 June 2017, https://www.aviva.com/newsroom/news-releases/2017/06/uk-six-million-uk-adults-dont-know-any-of-their-neighbours-by-name-17786/ (accessed 18 December 2023).

17 Kwiyani, *Multicultural Kingdom*, Chapter 10.

18 Christopher James, *Church Planting in Post-Christian Soil: Theology and practice* (OUP USA, 2018).

19 James, *Church Planting in Post-Christian Soil*, p. 227. 'Ecclesiopraxis' simply means how we do church.

20 Cathy Ross, 'Hospitality: The Church as Mother with an Open Heart' in Steve Bevans and Cathy Ross (eds), *Mission on the Road to Emmaus: Constants, context and prophetic dialogue* (London: SCM Press, 2015), p. 67.

21 Paul Keeble, *Mission With: Something out of the ordinary* (Instant Apostle, 2017).

22 William Lane, *The Gospel of Mark: New International Commentary* (Grand Rapids: MI: Wm. B. Eerdmans Publishing Co., 1974), p. 103.

23 'New research reveals family dinnertime is on the decline with only 28% of households sharing the same meal', *Sainsbury's*, 2021, https://www.about.sainsburys.co.uk/news/latest-news/2021/12-01-21-new-research-reveals-family-dinnertime (accessed 18 December 2023).

24 David W. Scott, Daryl R. Ireland, Grace Y. May and Casely B. Essamuah, *Unlikely Friends: How God Uses Boundary-Crossing Friendships to Transform the World* (Eugene, OR: Pickwick Publications, 2021), p. 159.

25 Kwiyani, *Multicultural Kingdom*, p. 77.

26 Donald Anderson McGavran, *The Bridges of God: A study in the strategy of missions* (Oregon: Wipf and Stock Publishers, 2005).

27 Miroslav Volf, *Exclusion and Embrace: A theological exploration of identity, otherness and reconciliation* (Abingdon Press, 2019), p. 26.

28 Tom Greggs, *Dogmatic Ecclesiology: The priestly catholicity of the church* (Baker Academic, 2019), p. 44.

29 Ben Lindsay, *We Need to Talk about Race: Understanding the Black experience in White majority churches* (London: SPCK, 2019); Kwiyani, *Multicultural Kingdom*.

30 Volf, *Exclusion and Embrace*, p. 46.

31 Volf, *Exclusion and Embrace*, p. 43.

32 Stefan Paas, *Experimenting with Mission and Unity in Secular Europe* in John Gibaut and Knud Jorgensen (eds), *Called to Unity for the Sake of Mission* (Oxford: Regnum Books International, 2014), p. 186.

33 John Wesley, *Catholic Spirit*, Sermon XXXIV in *John Wesley's Forty-Four Sermons* (Epworth Press, 1944), p. 451.

Chapter 5 – Church as witness

1 John Finney, *Recovering the Past: Celtic and Roman Mission* (London: Darton, Longman and Todd, 2011).

2 Newbigin, *Proper Confidence*, p. 76.

3 Kavin Rowe, 'The Ecclesiology of Acts' in David Goodhew (ed.), *Towards a Theology of Church Growth* (Surrey, England: 2015), p. 78.

4 Rowe, 'The Ecclesiology of Acts', p. 88.

5 John Colwell, *Living the Christian Story: The Distinctiveness of Christian Ethics* (New York: T&T Clark, 2001), p. 85.

6 Greg Okesson, *A Public Missiology: How local churches witness to a complex world* (Grand Rapids MI: Baker Academic, 2020), p. 24.

7 Okesson, *A Public Missiology*, p. 102.

8 Quoted in James Bratt (ed.), *Abraham Kuyper: A Centennial Reader* (Grand Rapids: Wm. B. Eerdmans, 1998), p. 488.

9 Newbigin, *Truth to Tell*, p. 89.

10 'Refugee Data Finder: 110 million forcibly displaced people worldwide', *UNHCR*, 24 October 2023, https://www.unhcr.org/refugee-statistics/ (accessed 18 December 2023).

11 Newbigin, *Proper Confidence,* p. 65.

12 Thomas King, *The Truth About Stories: A Native Narrative* (House of Anansi Press Inc, 2003).

13 Thomas King, 'The 2003 CBC Massey Lectures: The Truth About Stories: A Native Narrative', *CBC*, 7 November 2003.

14 Cited in Walter Hooper, *Past Watchful Dragons: The Narnian Chronicles of C. S. Lewis* (Macmillan Publishing Co., 1979), p. 37.

15 Brian Stone, *Evangelism After Christendom: The theology and practice of Christian witness* (Grand Rapids MI: Brazos Press, 2007), p. 38.

16 Newbigin, *Truth to Tell*, p. 94.

17 'Talking Jesus: 2022 Research Report', *Talking Jesus*, p. 18–9, https://talkingjesus.org/wp-content/uploads/2023/08/Talking-Jesus-Report-A4-AUG-23-WEB.pdf (accessed 18 December 2023).

18 Alexis Jay et al, 'Inquiry into Child Sexual Abuse in the Church of England and Wales: The Anglican Church Investigation Report', IICSA, October 2020, https://www.iicsa.org.uk/reports-recommendations/publications/investigation/anglican-church (accessed 7 January 2024).

19 Harvey C. Kwiyani, *Sent Forth: African Missionary Work in the West* (Orbis Books, 2014), p. 189.

20 Alpha, Pilgrim and Christianity Explored are all good introductory courses to the Christian Faith.

21 Harriet Sherwood, 'Why is the Christian population of England and Wales declining?' *The Guardian*, 29 November 2022, https://www.theguardian.com/world/2022/nov/29/

why-is-the-christian-population-of-england-and-wales-declining (accessed 7 January 2024); 'Religion, England and Wales: Census 2021', *ONS*.

22 Ed Thornton, 'Proposal to axe experts could affect hundreds of closures, warns church-rescuing charity', *Church Times*, 13 October 2021; Rebecca Paveley, 'Monthly churchgoing suits worshippers post-Covid, *Church Times*, 3 December 2021; 'GS 2222 – Church of England Mission in Revision: A review of the Mission and Pastoral Measure 2011', *Church of England,* June 2021, https://www.churchofengland.org/sites/default/files/2021-06/gs-2222-mission-in-revision-a-review-of-the-mission-and-pastoral-measure-2011.pdf (accessed 18 December 2023).

23 Quoted in Abigail Buchanan, 'Could Gen Z save the Church of England?', *The Telegraph*, 23 April 2023.

24 Pierre Babin and Mercedes Iannone, *The New Era of Religious Communication* (Minneapolis: Fortress, 1991), p. 196.

Chapter 6 – Church as dependent

1 John Taylor, *The Go-Between God: The Holy Spirit and the Christian Mission* (London: SCM Press, 1972), p. 4.

2 Taylor, *The Go-Between God*, p. 85.

3 Roland Allen, *Missionary Methods: St Paul's or ours?* (James Clarke and Co Ltd, Revised Edition, 2006).

4 Allen, *Missionary Methods*, p. 145.

5 Amos Yong, *Mission After Pentecost: The Witness of the Spirit from Genesis to Revelation* (Grand Rapids MI: Baker Academic, 2019).

6 Taylor, *The Go-Between God*, p. 111.

7 Taylor, *The Go-Between God*, p. 135.

8 Taylor, *The Go-Between God*, p. 147–8.

9 Lesslie Newbigin, *Mission in Christ's Way: A gift, a command, an assurance* (Friendship Press, 1988), p. 21.

10 William Abraham, *The Art of Evangelism: Evangelism carefully crafted into the life of the church* (Cliff College Publishing, 1993), p. 37.

11 Taylor, *The Go-Between God*, p. 19.

12 Yong, *Mission After Pentecost*, p. 137.

13 Okesson, *Public Missiology*, p. 89.

14 Yong, *Mission After Pentecost*, p. 179.

15 T. S. Eliot, 'Choruses to the Rock', *The Complete Poems and Plays* (London: Faber & Faber), p. 134.

16 Giles Fraser, 'The migrants' church in Calais is a place of raw prayer and defiant hope', *The Guardian*, 7 August 2015.

17 Hans Kung, *The Church* (London: Burns and Oates, 1967), p. 131.

18 'Meeting God at Glastonbury', *Diocese of Gloucester*, 23 May 2022, https://gloucester.anglican.org/2022/meeting-god-at-glastonbury/ (accessed 18 December 2023).

19 Paul Barnett, *The Birth of Christianity: the first twenty years* (Grand Rapids MI: Wm. B. Eerdmans Publishing, 2005), p. 8.

20 For more on this, see a chapter I wrote entitled 'Rooted and Sent: Generous Orthodoxy as an Expression of the Mission of God' in Nathan Eddy and Graham Tomlin (eds), *The Bond of Peace: Exploring generous orthodoxy* (London: SPCK, 2021).

21 Austen Ivereigh, 'An Interview with Pope Francis: A Time of Great Uncertainty', *Commonweal Magazine*, May 2020.

22 Andrew Walker, 'Recovering Deep Church' in Luke Bretherton and Andrew Walker (eds), *Remembering Our Future: Explorations in Deep Church* (London: Paternoster Press, 2007), p. 17.

23 Leonard I. Sweet, *Soul Tsunami: Sink or Swim in the new millennium culture* (Grand Rapids, MI: Zondervan, 1999), p. 17.

24 Alan J. Roxburgh, *Missional: Joining God in the neighbourhood* (Grand Rapids: Baker Books, 2011), p. 150.

25 Yong, *Mission After Pentecost*, p. 197.

26 Taylor, *The Go-Between God*, p. 234.

27 Taylor, *The Go-Between God*, p. 234.

28 Bob Hurley, *Living Outside the Box: A Peckham parable* (Bath: Comfort Books, 2006), p. 16.

29 Hurley, *Living Outside the Box*, p. 20.

Printed in the USA
CPSIA information can be obtained
at www.ICGtesting.com
CBHW050830120524
8391CB00007B/24

9 780281 087266